Also in the Star Book for Ministers series

Available now:
*The Star Book for Ministers*
Edward T. Hiscox

*The Star Book for Ministers* Gift Edition
Edward T. Hiscox

*The Star Book on Preaching*
Marvin A. McMickle

Coming soon…
*The Star Book for Pastoral Counseling*
Jason Richard Curry

# *The* *STAR BOOK* *for* *STEWARDSHIP*

★


**By**
**Clifford A. Jones Sr.**

**Kathryn V. Stanley, editor**

The Star Book for Stewardship


Throughout this book there are numerous references to individuals, church members, family, friends, and some thirty plus years of their wisdom sayings. Whenever and wherever possible I give direct reference, in others they are mentioned generally.



Interior design by Wendy Ronga / Cover design by Danny Ellison.

Library of Congress Cataloging-in-Publication data
Jones, Clifford A. The star book for stewardship / Clifford A. Jones, Sr. ; Kathryn V. Stanley, editor. p. cm.
ISBN 978-0-8170-1665-4 (hardback: alk. paper) 1. Christian giving—Handbooks, manuals, etc. 2. Christian stewardship—Handbooks, manuals, etc. I. Stanley, Kathryn V. II. Title.
BV772.J59 2012
248'.6—dc23 2011051584
Printed in the U.S.A.
First Edition, 2012.

# Preface

*The Star Book for Stewardship* is a call for practical biblical integrity to give contributions in honor of God as Creator—a call to responsively address disparities, which exist globally, by providing required resources. This can be achieved through facility usage, advocacy for the victimized, food for the hungry, and shelters for the homeless.

This book is much more than meeting church budgets and waiting with open hands for divine reciprocity, dollar-for-dollar. This volume approaches stewardship as a lifestyle encompassing responsiveness to community needs, management of personal resources, and worship through giving tithes and offerings—as responsible stewards and disciples of the Lord Jesus Christ.

*The Star Book for Stewardship* is a personal and pastoral presentation about giving with positive attitudes reflected through informed community outreach. If religious organizations, especially the church, are to have successful benevolent and receiving ministries, leadership must model what it is to give and receive tithes and contributions. This presentation is broader than blessing the person of God, sowing seeds into ministry, and developing financial wealth strategies.

Stewardship is approached from a pre-Mosaic law period and post-Pauline theological perspective rooted in honoring God, embracing responsibility for one's neighbor, and providing tangible and spiritual inspiration, guidance, and hope. In his biography, *Up from Slavery*, Booker T. Washington said, "I have found that the happiest people are those who do the most for others; the most miserable are those who do least" (p. 229). This book is about making ourselves and others more useful and, thereby, happy.

Ecclesiastical thievery—as manifested by individuals, churches, associations, conventions, and denominations—results in complacency in addressing human needs. It is an inability to sustain historical institutions, churches, assembly grounds, and religious schools. Whenever individuals and institutions refuse to honor God through giving tithes and offerings, God is robbed of glory rightfully due, as are those who are in need of rightful assistance.

God's kingdom on earth deserves our best at all times; a hurting humanity deserves more. Creation is growing in agony because of our neglect; streams and rivers are weeping polluted tears; congested air has an infectious cough; and scared forests are bending beneath eons of abuse. Certainly, all of God's creation deserves so much more.

For all these reasons, *The Star Book for Stewardship* is about more than increasing the church's financial position or providing a guide to personal wealth acquisition, although godly stewardship is likely to influence each of these goals.

Fundamentally, this book is a biblical, pastoral, and personal experiential approach to honoring God for blessings received through expressions of thanksgiving: giving tithes and contributions. It is a stewardship covenant to intentionally move those who say *no* to *I believe* and, ultimately, *yes*!

# Acknowledgments

*The Star Book for* Stewardship combines forty years of wisdom collected from a host of individuals, churches, associations, conventions, and denominations. Before I ever opened a book about stewardship, I developed an appreciation for numerous practices and traditions churches have used to nurture congregants in the faith while keeping their lights on. Raffles, twelve tribe rallies, bake sales, fish dinners, penny offerings, pledging, and tithes and offerings are not only fundraising tactics, but they also present opportunities for fellowship and friendly competition to raise money.

I am eternally grateful to First Baptist Church, Florence Estates in Berlin, New Jersey, where I grew up, for nurturing me in the faith; Aeon Baptist Church, Rochester, New York, where I preached my initial sermon; the first two churches where I served as pastor: Bethlehem Baptist Church and Brookstone Baptist Church in Carthage, North Carolina and Greystone, North Carolina, respectively; my first full-time church employer, First Baptist Church in Clinton, North

Carolina; and Friendship Missionary Baptist Church in Charlotte, North Carolina, where I have served as pastor for more than twenty-nine years. Your love and support over the years have been a tremendous blessing.

My wife, Brenda, has been supportive and caring and urged me to write; her faith has been a stable support for my ministry. Thank you! To all my children, my precious jewels, know you bring immeasurable joy to my life.

To the Friendship Missionary Baptist Church staff, you make it possible for me to be involved in global ministry. Thank you for your loyalty and diligent work.

I also extend my appreciation to Sandra Chapman and Nancy Stroud of First Legacy Credit Union, as well as Rita Franklin and Carla Patterson for laboring to bring this manuscript into fruition.

Most of all, I thank the Spirit of the universe for providing the experiences along life's journey that enable me to write using collective memories. I fervently pray these pages bring ultimate glory to God's kingdom and stimulate the will among God's people to provide resources for the least of God's children.

# Introduction

For centuries, the concept of Christian stewardship has garnered attention from the pulpit and pew alike. Its meaning and requirements have been, and continue to be, the source of great discussion and debate. Two consistently disputed principles are whether the concept of tithing is limited to the Old Testament and whether it should be based on gross or net income.

Those tasked with the responsibility of teaching the meaning and application of Christian stewardship often tread lightly on the topic for fear of alienating seemingly faithful members of their congregations. Yet I assert the foundation of Christian stewardship is faith itself.

German theologian Helmut Thielicke wrote: "Stewardship doesn't begin with obligation. Stewardship doesn't being with legality. Stewardship doesn't begin with fear. Stewardship doesn't begin with desire for gain. Stewardship begins with mastery…the making of Christ Lord and Master of our lives."[1] Therefore, teaching designed to foster the discipline of giving is built upon leading people into a deeper relationship with the Giver of all things.

Hopefully, *The Star Book for Stewardship* will help church leadership stimulate congregant desires to strengthen their individual faith walk with God as Creator and Sustainer, and honor God through tithing. It will be the ultimate manifestation of this strengthened relationship. Additionally, this volume seeks to strengthen the congregational witness so it will become an advocate for the poor and oppressed as part of their global stewardship.

This book is intended as a practical guide to personal and institutional stewardship—a primer for individuals, religious leaders (lay and clergy), and churches as communal bodies. "Part I: Biblical Foundations for Stewardship," explores the foundations of biblical stewardship throughout Scripture.

Part II: Practicing Christian Stewardship discusses practical principles of Christian stewardship, and Part III: The Church as Steward suggests that effective stewardship in Christian institutions requires churches to exercise transparency and financial accountability, as well as fulfill its responsibility to meet the needs of the poor.

Part IV: Preaching & Teaching discusses the transformative power of the biblical principles of stewardship taught through preaching, teaching, serving, and participating in the fellowship of the community of the faithful. This section includes monthly meditations and sermon outlines designed to move individuals and congregations from membership to discipleship, from discipleship to stewardship.

Finally, Part V: Worship Tools provides testimonies from clergy and laity who have fully embraced Christian stewardship as a way of life.

Note

1. Helmut Thielicke, *The Waiting Father: Sermons on the Parables of Jesus* (New York: Harper and Brothers, 1959), 51.

S E C T I O N I

# Biblical Foundations for Stewardship

Holy Scripture provides the basis for giving and is the standard for analyzing the authenticity of written stewardship material. The biblical basis for tithing and all aspects of stewardship is securely nestled in a belief in God, who is the ultimate Giver and Owner of everything, including human life. All humanity lives because of divine generosity. Any form of giving is, at best, returning to God what he has entrusted in our care.

Human activity exists only in the realm of God. All Scripture is built on this premise: "In the beginning when God created" (Genesis 1:1). Before we commence any discussion about giving, we must yield to the following fundamental premise as recorded in Genesis 1:26-28:

> Then God said, "Let us make humankind in our image, according to our likeness; and let them have dominion over the fish of the sea, and over the birds of the air, and over the cattle, and over

> all the wild animals of the earth, and over every creeping thing that creeps upon the earth." So God created humankind in his image, in the image of God he created them; male and female he created them. God blessed them, and God said to them, "Be fruitful and multiply, and fill the earth and subdue it; and have dominion over the fish of the sea and over the birds of the air and over every living thing that moves upon the earth."[1]

With this premise in mind, this chapter argues that the concept of stewardship, specifically tithing, is present throughout the biblical witness. It predates Mosaic law; was codified by all the Law and the Prophets; affirmed through the life, death, and resurrection of Jesus Christ; and was ultimately a tenet of the early church.

## 1. The Pre-Mosaic Period

The tithe—one-tenth of property or produce (crops or herds), usually given to support religious institutions and the priesthood—was commonly known during ancient times. "Tithing was an ancient and widespread practice; reference to it is found in other religions and cultures than those of Israel or the Semitic peoples alone."[2]

References to tithing in the Bible are reflective of various customs and different historical periods and places. While it is almost impossible to pinpoint its exact origins, it is clear that tithing was an ancient, pre-Mosaic law practice and was the expected starting point as a return for God's grace.

The first mention of the concept occurs in Genesis 14. In this chapter, a tithe was given from Abram to Melchizedek, a high priest, who in that day was considered the mediator between God and the people, as an expression of gratitude and thanksgiving:

> And King Melchizedek of Salem brought out bread and wine; he was priest of God Most High. He blessed him and said, "Blessed be Abram by God Most High, maker of heaven and earth; and blessed be God Most High, who has delivered your enemies into your hand!" And Abram gave him one tenth of everything.
> (Genesis 14:18-20)

A second pre-Mosaic passage on tithing is also recorded in the book of Genesis. It occurs in the account of Jacob's encounter with God at Bethel. In this text, Jacob bargained with God—if God blessed him, Jacob would give God the tithe:

> Then Jacob made a vow, saying, "If God will be with me, and will keep me in this way that I go, and will give me bread to eat and clothing to wear, so that I come again to my father's house in peace, then the LORD shall be my God, and this stone, which I have set up for a pillar, shall be God's house; and of all that you give me I will surely give one tenth to you." (Genesis 28:20-22)

In both of these pre-Mosaic law passages the tithe is given in response to God's goodness. In the text, Abram presents a gift of thanksgiving to God through the priest. For Jacob, it is given in response to God's graciousness. The tenth was holy unto the Lord God: Creator and Redeemer.

**The Law and Prophets**

The Law of the Old Testament was undergirded by the recognition of God as Creator and Owner of all. The tithe was made in faith as an act of thanksgiving to honor God: "All tithes from the land, whether the seed from the ground or the fruit from the tree, are the LORD'S; they are holy to the LORD" (Leviticus 27:30).

The Old Testament is replete with references to the appropriate gift given to the Creator by God's people, who are caretakers, inhabitants, recipients, trustees, and stewards of God's creation. God's people were taught and expected to give the tithe.[3] Indeed, because the tithe was given for a number of purposes in Deuteronomy at regular and special intervals, it has been speculated that the annual tithe could amount to as much as 20 percent, and on each third year, even as much as 30 percent.

The tithe, contributions, and first fruit offerings of grain, oil, wine, and cattle were given at designated places and times to God through the priesthood as an offer of thanksgiving and for the poor and their sustenance. The Israelites understood any accumulation of wealth was a direct result of God's graciousness.

Tithing is codified in the Mosaic law beginning in the book of Deuteronomy. The book commanded tithing in two circumstances. First, the tithe, one-tenth of the agricultural yield, was to be used in celebration of Passover, Feast of Tabernacles, and Feast of Weeks. These offerings included the sacrificial meal shared in the household:

> Set apart a tithe of all the yield of your seed that is brought in yearly from the field. In the presence of the LORD your God, in the place that he will choose as a dwelling for his name, you shall eat the tithe of your grain, your wine, and your oil, as well as the firstlings of your herd and flock, so

> that you may learn to fear the LORD your God always. (Deuteronomy 14:22-23)

This first reference emphasizes giving as a part of spiritual discipline that reverences God.

The second manner in which tithe is referenced in Deuteronomy relates to its support of people in need—the Levites, sojourner, fatherless, and widow—who did not own land or have the wherewithal to provide for themselves:

> As for the Levites resident in your towns, do not neglect them, because they have no allotment or inheritance with you. Every third year you shall bring out the full tithe of your produce for that year, and store it within your towns; the Levites, because they have no allotment or inheritance with you, as well as the resident aliens, the orphans, and the widows in your towns, may come and eat their fill so that the LORD your God may bless you in all the work that you undertake. (Deuteronomy 14:27-29)[4]

Tithing in the Old Testament cultivated a generous spirit, especially as it was extended to the poor. Scripture teaches God delighted in the spirit of giving:

> Happy are those who consider the poor;
> the LORD delivers them in the day of trouble.
> The LORD protects them and keeps them alive;
> they are called happy in the land.
> You do not give them up to the will of their
> enemies.
> The LORD sustains them on their sickbed;
> in their illness you heal all their infirmities.
> —Psalm 41:1-3

The intent of tithing, both in pre-Mosaic law and throughout the Old Testament, far exceeds mere legalism as the reason for giving. Tithing honored God and responded to the needs of the people. However, there were times when the prophets made a call to the people of God when they became unresponsive to the needs of the people and the house of God.

Prophets posed questions such as: "Why is the house of God forsaken?"(Nehemiah 13:11) or "Will anyone rob God?"(Malachi 3:8). As he installed the Levites to their posts, Nehemiah said: "Then all Judah brought the tithe of the grain, wine, and oil into the storehouses" (Nehemiah 13:12).

There is also the passionate appeal of Malachi: "Bring the full tithe into the storehouse, so that there may be food in my house, and thus put me to the test, says the LORD of hosts; see if I will not open the windows of heaven for you and pour down for you an overflowing blessing" (3:10). Like a pleading mother to a straying child, Malachi taught bringing the tithe in honor of God, with the promise that God will supply the people's needs accordingly. Malachi even challenged the people to put God, the sustainer of all, to the test.

David exalts the joy of tithing as returning to God as owner of all things: "Now, our God, we give thanks to you and praise your glorious name. But who am I, and what is my people, that we should be able to make this freewill offering? For all things come from you, and of your own have we given you" (1 Chronicles 29:13-14).

Giving in the Old Testament was a practice to honor God and provide sustenance for those in need. Giving was not practiced as a means of receiving or getting from God, but was recognition of divine ownership. For us, it is an affirmation of our utter dependence on God.

Giving acknowledges that we are created in God's image. Therefore, it is our character to give and live. We must live an accountable and responsible lifestyle as a steward of a sacred trust. Our understanding of and faith in God informs our giving. Authentic religious transformation informs not only our relationship with God, but also our relationship to those who need what God has entrusted to us.

As the crown jewel of creation, neither male nor female was given one centimeter of earth to own. We are merely caretakers, stewards, managers, and trustees of God's creation. A sober and humble biblical perspective recognizes that humans belong to God and have been created to live in relation to all creation. We, and all we have accumulated, are ultimately God's possessions.

Douglas Johnson, author of *Tithe: Challenge or Legalism*, wrote: "The spiritual message of the Old Testament is that people have been given creation as a trust and they are expected to manage it for God."[5] The belief in divine ownership of all possessions belonging to God finds expression through tithes, offering of first fruits, and contributions for those in need.

Responsiveness to others and God was a way of life, not something merely practiced during festive seasons and worship. Tithing, contributions, and first fruit offerings were practiced by stewards, caretakers, managers, and trustees—recipients of God's gifts. Responding to a gracious God through giving was engrained into the culture's fabric.

Indeed, had giving only been a legal response, it would have been unacceptable and depreciated a person's relationship with God. Giving was a lifestyle. As recipients of God's best, it was expected for God to be honored with one's best: "Honor the LORD with your substance and with the first fruits of all your produce" (Proverbs 3:9).

It is right, it is always right to honor the Lord with the first fruits, tithes, and contributions—the very best of time, talents, influence, and service simply because God is God. How can we, whose lives are totally dependent upon God, dare to rob God? Receiving on one hand and robbing and holding back on the other is robbing God.

This practice can cause a breach in divine and human relationship. God continuously gives; we receive ad infinitum. We are blessed daily, sufficiently, and efficiently with all the essentials for today. How can we lapse into being what minister and civil rights activist Dr. Wyatt Tee Walker calls "common thieves"?

Listen carefully to the prophet Malachi:

> Will anyone rob God? Yet you are robbing me! But you say, "How are we robbing you?" In your tithes and offerings! You are cursed with a curse, for you are robbing me—the whole nation of you! Bring the full tithe into the storehouse, so that there may be food in my house, and thus put

> me to the test, says the LORD of hosts; see if I will not open the windows of heaven for you and pour down for you an overflowing blessing. (Malachi 3:8-10 NRSV)

In these verses, Malachi is not castigating the people for not paying assessments and dues or failing to be generous servants of God. Nor is he scolding them for a lack of attentiveness to facility maintenance and upkeep, or for neglecting deferred and endowment giving. He is not even calling attention to responsiveness for the poor, the homeless, widows, and victims of social injustice.

For sure, all the aforementioned are worthy reasons for giving. Rather, Malachi's words are a clear, unyielding indictment upon our honor to God as Creator, Provider, and Sustainer of life through our tithes and offerings.

The purposes prescribed for tithing in the Old Testament are still apropos for us today. First, our tithing indicates a genuine belief in God as ultimate Owner and Giver, and the community of the faith's willingness to honor God through the tithe. Second, our tithes assist the church in providing for the needs of the poor. God's call to tithe, then and now, reflects these Old Testament tenets.

## 2. Wisdom Literature

The book of Ecclesiastes contains a series of reflections on wealth, riches, money, property, fortunes, and possessions interspersed with personal philosophical directives. There are at least twenty-nine references to the aforementioned; of this number, eleven refer to wealth, ten to riches, and three to money.

The preacher in Ecclesiastes, who was king over Israel in Jerusalem, had access to great possessions, but could find neither satisfaction nor happiness from them. Therefore, he exclaimed: "Vanity of vanities, says the Teacher, vanity of vanities! All is vanity. What do people gain from all the toil at which they toil under the sun?" (Ecclesiastes 1:2-3).

*Vanity* is a translation of a Hebrew expression of the utter insufficiency of all earthly things to cause or perpetuate one's happiness. The New International Version of the Bible translates vanity in Ecclesiastes 1:2-3 as "Meaningless, meaningless!" According to Old Testament scholar Reverend Dr. R.B.Y. Scott in the *Anchor Bible*, Ecclesiastes 1:1 can also be expanded and translated: "Vanity of vanities, all is vanity can freely be expanded to, 'everything in life is hollow and utterly futile; it is the thinnest of vapors, fleeting as a breath and amounts to nothing'" (p. 198).

The fruitlessness of human efforts is to attain happiness illustrated in Ecclesiastes 1:3-11, through references to changes in the natural order. Things are mutable, change is continual, circumstances are inconsistent; life is restless in the midst of opulence. Life just isn't fair.

The teacher seemingly advocates enjoying life because our days are short and old age overtakes us, not in an ostentatious manner for this, too, is meaningless. Do good deeds and balance work and leisure. Exercise restraint and self-control: "Sometimes one who has toiled with wisdom and knowledge and skill must leave all to be enjoyed by another who did not toil for it. This also is vanity and a great evil" (Ecclesiastes 2:21).

Ecclesiastes is replete with warnings about work, leisure, and possessions. Chapter 5, offers the complaint of one who worked only to lose everything in a business venture in verses 13-17, and chapter 6 illustrates a person who accumulated vast wealth but lacked the power to enjoy it in verses 1-6. The teacher draws conclusions that religious stewards must ponder:

1. Earthly possessions cannot possibly make a person truly happy (see Ecclesiastes 12:8).

2. Divine wisdom alone can teach us to make the best of life while living in an imperfect world (see Ecclesiastes 12:9-12).

3. Cultivate submissive reverence for our Creator (see Ecclesiastes 12:13).

4. Live with the expectation that one has a future state of existence after old age if one trusts in God (see Ecclesiastes 12:14).

## 3. The New Testament

**The Gospels**

The New Testament affirms the Hebrew understanding of the sovereignty of God as Creator, Ruler, and Sustainer. Christian stewardship is based on this understanding. In the Gospel according to John we read:

> In the beginning was the Word, and the Word was with God, and the Word was God. He was in the beginning with God. All things came into being through him, and without him not one thing came into being. What has come into being in him was life, and the life was the light of all people. The light shines in the darkness, and the darkness did not overcome it.... The Word became flesh and lived among us, and we have seen his glory, the glory as of a father's only son, full of grace and truth. (John 1:1-5,14)

The New Testament affirms the divine creation and God as the benefactor of all who dwell in the divinely created order. Christian stewardship, as understood in New Testament, includes responsible management of the created order and its resources, as well as responsible management as stewards of the Good News of Jesus the Christ.

Without question, Christian stewardship recognizes the call for accountability to one's trusted guardianship of land, clean air, and water: fowl of the air, fishes of the sea, and all living things. However, Christian stewardship also emphasizes accountability for the poor, the hungry, victims of social injustice, the homeless, and advocacy for the rights of women and children. We are responsible for our neighbors. We are our brothers' and sisters' keepers.

Therefore, Christian stewardship does not end with the tithe and contribution in the offering baskets. It includes the love and care of everything God has brought into existence.

A Christian steward relinquishes his or her personal agenda, privileges, and rights. When one becomes a believer, how faith is practiced defines the believer's life. This understanding is the basis of Dr. Walker's belief that, "We are trustees, never owners."[6] We are Christian caretakers of God's creation, including ourselves.

Professor, author, and New Testament Scholar A.R. Fagan said, "There is a cosmological as well as eschatological issue of accountability by the owner."[7] Ignoring people in need appallingly affects our witness as believers. Consequently, it affects our eternal destiny. This concept is validated in Matthew 25:44-46:

> Then they also will answer, "Lord, when was it that we saw you hungry or thirsty or a stranger or naked or sick or in prison, and did not take care of you?" Then he will answer them, "Truly I tell you, just as you did not do it to one of the least of these, you did not do it to me." And these will go away into eternal punishment, but the righteous into eternal life.[8]

Christian stewards have responsibility for all of creation as guardians, caretakers, and our brothers' and sisters' keepers. The Creator will ultimately hold each of us accountable for our use of our God-given resources. Our hands and arms, our influence and affluence, our prayers and petitions, our tithe and time; and our work and witness are needed.

Again, the words of Fagan prove to be helpful:

> It is the position of the biblical material, the New Testament assumes it from the Old Testament and

> builds on it, that all substance and circumstances are so because God made them or permits them to be so. This is the Christian Doctrine of Creation. The Christian is aware that his substance (chemical, physical and fabricated) and his circumstances (temporal, geographical, etc.) must be related to God in Christ through the Holy Spirit. This is the Doctrine of Stewardship. It involves how man uses resources and where he spends his time.[9]

The Bible teaches that giving to honor God is also a means of being responsible for the needs of others. While Caesar compels giving, Jesus—with compelling encouragement—invites giving in Matthew 22:21: "Give therefore to the emperor the things that are the emperor's, and to God the things that are God's." The wisdom of Jesus acknowledged the local law and recognized the image on Roman coinage. Additionally, it called for faithfulness to the ultimate image in which we are all created, the image of God.

Psalm 8:3-9 says it well:

> When I look at your heavens, the work of
> your fingers,
> the moon and the stars that you have
> established;

what are human beings that you are mindful
of them,
mortals that you care for them?
Yet you have made them a little lower than God,
and crowned them with glory and honor.
You have given them dominion over the works
of your hands;
you have put all things under their feet,
all sheep and oxen, and also the beasts of
the field,
the birds of the air, and the fish of the sea,
whatever passes along the paths of the seas.
O LORD, our Sovereign, how majestic is
your name in all the earth!

Following Jesus Christ as Lord and Savior requires complete loyalty and dedication. Loyal discipleship demands giving beyond the tithe; dedicated discipleship leads to a serious personal rethinking about the limitation of tithing.

For Christians, giving of the tithe is the springboard for a much higher expectation. As followers of Christ, giving—in honor of God and to meet the needs of the poor—is now driven by a spirit of grace, not demanded by commandments of law.

Jesus has become the benchmark for understanding

giving. Now followers live not by the letter of law, but by the Spirit of Christ. Christians acknowledge one's obligation and duty is to model Christ's example of giving. New Testament scholar Frank Stagg wrote: "As a voluntary system, tithing offers much; but it must be redeemed by grace if it is to be Christian. To plead that it works is only to adopt the pragmatic tests of the world, 'much works' that is not Christian. Tithing, if it is to be congenial to New Testament theology, must be rooted in the grace and love of God."[10]

Jesus Christ sought with gracious teachings to move a religious mindset of legalism to one of grace. He did not deny the law as an acceptable practice, nor did he deny it as unacceptable. Rather, Jesus understood the Old Testament teaching of tithing as the beginning of Christian giving.

Christ challenged his followers about the necessity of honoring God, by being caring and responsive to the poor by living beyond the letter of law to living a life of total commitment to all he or she is or has. To be sure, Jesus did not wish to eliminate the law. In fact, he declared:

> *Do not think that I have come to abolish the law or the prophets; I have come not to abolish but to fulfill.* For truly I tell you, until heaven and earth pass away, not one letter, not one stroke of

> a letter, will pass from the law until all is accomplished. Therefore, whoever breaks one of the least of these commandments, and teaches others to do the same, will be called least in the kingdom of heaven; but whoever does them and teaches them will be called great in the kingdom of heaven. For I tell you, unless your righteousness exceeds that of the scribes and Pharisees, you will never enter the kingdom of heaven. (Matthew 5:17-20, emphasis added)

Jesus pushes for more from his followers; something beyond the one-tenth the law requires. Jesus requires us to examine motive, attitude, purpose, and will with respect to living and giving while acknowledging the practice of tithing as worthy and needful. He states: "Woe to you, scribes and Pharisees, hypocrites! For you tithe mint, dill, and cumin, and have neglected the weightier matters of the law: justice and mercy and faith. It is these you ought to have practiced without neglecting the others" (Matthew 23:23; see also Luke 11:42).

Jesus clearly recognizes and affirms the principle of tithing, and commends the practitioners for being so meticulous in giving the tithe of the smallest possession. Yet, he rightfully criticizes the Pharisees for following the law of the tithe without practicing the love that faith requires. Practicing justice, mercy, and faithfulness authenticates the tithe. Without the former, tithing becomes a mere religious ritual.

The tithing of assets must be continuously reexamined to determine if it adheres to the law of love. The parable of the Pharisee and the tax collector in Luke 18 demonstrates Jesus' response to tithing in a way that is, again, not a condemnation of the act, but a call for humility before God:

> The Pharisee, standing by himself, was praying thus, "God, I thank you that I am not like other people: thieves, rogues, adulterers, or even like this tax collector. I fast twice a week; I give a tenth of all my income." But the tax collector, standing far off, would not even look up to heaven, but was beating his breast and saying, "God, be merciful to me, a sinner!" I tell you, this man went down to his home justified rather than the other; for all who exalt themselves will be humbled, but all who humble themselves will be exalted. (Luke 18:11-14)

These passages condemn displays of negative feelings toward God's people. Also condemned are displays of self-righteousness, and trust in personal merit. In no way, however, do these passages condemn tithing. Rather, Jesus' ministry demands believers practice humility before the Creator, not feeling privileged or preferred, righteous or arrogant, but humbly grateful. Responding to the divine call to give is not to the letter of the law but a humble appeal to God's free mercy.

Fagan said, if anyone "is ever to live life as God meant it to be lived, God's place of authority must be reestablished within the life of the individual."[11] Followers of Jesus Christ are admonished to live in such a manner that their chief assets would not be the accumulation of wealth, prestige, and power—all of which can be beneficial—but investments in things for others and one's eternal future.

Wyatt Tee Walker quoted an old epitaph, which reads: "What I gave I have, what I spent I had, what I kept I lost."[12] A story of a man is illustrated here, who was in debt for a large sum of money.

The man was approached by a friend who said, "Now, aren't you sorry you gave so much to the Lord?"

"No," the man said, "I am glad, for it is the only investment I made that is still paying dividends."

In general, discussions about stewardship, tithing, finances, attitudes, and giving are about reorienting one's lifestyle in a godly manner. The teachings of Jesus don't set one free from the biblical understanding of tithing. Rather, they move one who tithes to a conscious giving of self.

Douglas Johnson penned: "Some see the New Testament as not teaching the tithe, but one asks if the Christian should give less under grace than the Jews did under the law. The New Testament teaches that all of one's possessions belong to God. Did not the Old Testament do likewise?"[13]

**The Early Church and Epistles**

Stewardship was also a practice of the early church. Among the first Christians, people of the Way were mandated a change in attitude and practice about how personal possessions were to be regarded. According to Acts 4:32: "Now the whole group of those who believed were of one heart and soul, and no one claimed private ownership of any possessions, but everything they owned was held in common."

Since those first believers in Jesus were primarily Jewish, it seems safe to assume tithing was their starting point for giving. However, after becoming part of the new community of disciples who followed the Way, their regular and systematic giving of the tithe seems to transition beyond any notion of personal possession at all.

Christians need a standard for honoring God's redemptive act in Jesus Christ. As recipients of God's grace, which was ultimately evidenced through the sacrifice of Jesus Christ, tithing is the minimal standard for the believer. This affirmation makes all giving a response to grace. Offerings in the early church were purposeful acts of grace, designed to provide care for widows and orphans, as well as aid to those in need of food and other essentials.

In the early church, the standard for giving is revealed in the stewardship practices of Paul and the other apostles. Before his conversion experience, Paul was Saul, a Pharisee who practiced the law: "I am a Jew, born in Tarsus of Cilicia, but brought up in this city at the feet of Gamaliel, educated strictly according to our ancestral law, being zealous for God, just as all of you are today.... While I was on my way and approaching Damascus, about noon a great light from heaven suddenly shone about me" (Acts 22:3,6).

In Acts 26:5, Paul declared, "They have known for a long time, if they are willing to testify, that I belonged to the strictest sect of our religion and lived as a Pharisee." Later, in Philippians 3:4-6, he said, "If anyone else has reason to be confident in the flesh, I have more: circumcised on the eighth day, a member of the people of Israel, of the tribe of Benjamin, a Hebrew born of Hebrews; as to the law, a Pharisee; as to zeal, a persecutor of the church; as to righteousness under the law, blameless."

For Paul, the foundation for Christian stewardship is founded not only in an understanding of the Law, but also in God's revelation through Jesus Christ. A Christian is the recipient of divine generosity. All giving is rooted and springs forth from this rich soil. In 1 Corinthians 6:19-20, Paul expressed this understanding to the Corinthians when he said, "Do you not know that your body is a temple of the Holy Spirit within you, which you have from God, and that you are not your own? For you were bought with a price; therefore glorify God in your body."

Paul, who was nurtured, formally-educated, and religiously trained as a Pharisee by faith and practice, would have known and practiced tithing. Further, after his conversion experience, there is no indication he ever spoke or taught against tithing. Indeed, he lauded young believers of Macedonia for their demonstration of God's grace through their generosity: "Their extreme poverty have overflowed in a wealth of generosity on their part. For, as I can testify, they voluntarily gave according to their means, and even beyond their means" (2 Corinthians 8:2-3).

Believers no longer walk and live in darkness, but in the marvelous light. There is not any percentage of one's resources or of oneself that is deemed adequate. No amount is impoverishing if it is modeled after the giving of Jesus, who gave 100 percent for all, for all times. Therefore, Paul reminds us in 2 Corinthians 8:8-9: "I do not say this as a command, but I am testing the genuineness of your love against the earnestness of others. For you know the generous act of our Lord Jesus Christ, that though he was rich, yet for your sakes he became poor, so that by his poverty you might become rich."

The practice of biblical stewardship through tithing never impoverishes; it enriches a faith relationship to God, our Creator, and provides needed sustenance and empowerment for our sisters and brothers. A positive attitude about biblical stewardship is fostered through an authentic faith in God as Creator and Jesus Christ as Lord and Savior.

The early Christians were not people of wealth and means, but they did possess an abundance of joy, which moved them beyond earthly means to be abundantly generous to others. Giving enables us to trust a Savior, who gave all for us. He became poor so we could be rich.

While Paul clearly taught the necessity of stewardship, he did not teach the law of the tithe. This was due to a call of grace; he wanted to move the paradigm for giving by early Christians far beyond the letter of the law, which as a strict, transformed Pharisee, he knew all too well. Further, Paul encouraged setting aside a portion of one's resources for community needs, for those who had little or nothing. He encouraged believers who had little to share with joy.

It has become a kind of truism to say that all giving is local. Indeed, even in times of financial difficulty, when giving to international missions and global ministries tends to decrease, most of us are more willing to support local mission and ministry efforts. We like to see the effect closer to home, and that is good news for the pastor and preacher. After all, nothing is more local than the local church.

## 4. Conclusion

Any conclusive analysis of biblical stewardship and tithing must find its ultimate meaning and purpose in God—Owner, Creator, Sustainer—as well as in the redemptive act of Jesus. From this understanding of humanity—as the created, sustained, and redeemed—grows an increasing awareness of our responsibility as participants in the kingdom of God.

Tithing becomes meaningful, not for personal, reciprocal divine graces, but to urgently address the international status and needs of the poor, marginalized, hungry, powerless, and displaced. The global masses living on the periphery are personally challenged by their lack, but their lack is an even greater challenge for people of faith to determine how they will live faithfully with money.

Giving tithes and offerings should not be exclusively yoked to money. It is inadequately yoked if this is the case. Christians are called to embrace attitudes about giving that are representative of God's redemptive act through Jesus Christ. This giving is not simply of one's treasure, but also of one's time and talents.

These directives have not diminished or eroded throughout eons; they still remain requirements of those who say, "I believe." If individuals refuse to accept and practice the biblical directive to tithe, they miss a marvelous opportunity to discover God's presence in the larger arena of life. Even more, their refusal to be responsive as believers in the body of Christ is a refusal to be responsive to the least of these: our sisters and brothers in need.

Notes

1. See Genesis 2:7 (Breath of life); Genesis 2:15 (Placed in the garden of Eden by God); Genesis 3:19 (Humanity returns to the dust); 1 Chronicles 29:12 (Wealth and honor come from God); Job 14:1-2 (Mortals spring up and wither like

flowers); Psalm 8:1-9 (Made lower than heavenly beings); Psalm 90:1-2 (God is from everlasting to everlasting); Psalm 146:4 (Humanity returns to the ground); Ecclesiastes 3:21 (Human spirit rises upward); Ecclesiastes 12:7 (The dust returns to the ground); and Ezekiel 18:4 (All souls are God's).

2. *The Interpreter's Dictionary of the Bible*, Vol. 4. (Nashville: Abingdon Press, 1962), 654.

3. The tithe, being holy, was to be brought to the place and persons designated by the Lord and received by priests. In Numbers 18:21-32, the tithe was received by Levites for services, and from this the Levite was to give a tithe as an offering to the Lord.

4. See Deuteronomy 26:12-15.

5. Douglas W. Johnson, *The Tithe: Challenge or Legalism?* (Nashville: Abingdon Press, 1984), 29.

6. Wyatt Tee Walker, *Common Thieves! A Tithing Manual for Black Christians and Others* (New York: Martin Luther King Fellows Press, 1986), 11.

7. A.R. Fagan, *What the Bible Says about Stewardship* (Nashville: Convention Press, 1976), 8.

8. See Mark 13:32-37 (Servants in charge until he returns); Luke 12:37-48 (Lack of charity to the poor); Luke 19:11-26 (Failure to be trustworthy with divine resources); Romans 14:8 (We belong to the Lord); and Revelation 21:1-4 (God's dwelling is finally with us).

9. Fagan, *What the Bible Says about Stewardship*, 8.

10. Johnson, *The Tithe: Challenge or Legalism?*, 169.

11. Fagan, *What the Bible Says about Stewardship*, 15.

12. Walker, *Common Thieves*, 27.

13. Johnson, *TheTithe: Challenge or Legalism?*, 184.

S E C T I O N I I

# Practicing Christian Stewardship

Meditations and preaching are by all means essential to developing a congregation of stewards. Equally as important, however, are practical instructions for Christian stewardship. This section presents core values necessary to practice good Christian stewardship.

Christian stewardship, like yoga, is a spiritual practice. One overarching principle in the practice of yoga is strengthening the core or the abdomen area. The core is the place from which all other yoga exercises emanate.

In yoga, a key core-strengthening pose is downward facing dog. This pose, used constantly throughout yoga class, results in a strengthened core, which helps yoga practitioners become more flexible, have better posture, build stronger bodies, and experience better digestion, among other benefits.

Like yoga, Christian stewardship must be practiced. There are certain key or core values of Christian stewardship, which practitioners must embrace and engage to become strong in the discipline. A Christian steward is expected to manage the resources of this economy in a manner pleasing, not only by earthly standards, but also by divine expectations.

There are three important practices necessary for sound personal financial management. They are vital because practicing good Christian stewardship begins with managing the resources we are given. These practices are (1) debt reduction and management, (2) saving and giving, and (3) end-of-life planning. Finally, there is what I have coined piggy bank theology— stewardship practices we can instill in young people.

## 5. Debt Reduction and Management

Many Americans tend to live above their means; Christians are no different. We have more bills and debt than income and credit. We spend more money than we make. We engage in using credit cards to pay for daily expenses, without paying them off each month. These practices may result in debt management challenges.

Responsible Christian stewards must manage income and expenditures in a prudent and godly manner. As believers, we are accountable for managing the part of the earth God has entrusted to us. A personal debt reduction and management plan allows Christian stewards to reach financial and other goals, reduce household stress, as well as be in a position to contribute to the church and charitable organizations. In short, being released from debt allows us to enjoy the marvelous gift of life God intends for each of us.

Assisting with congregational debt management may require the church to enlist the services of experts in the area of debt management. There are a number of nonprofit organization with which the church may partner to facilitate debt management education and assistance. The church may also call for a congregational debt fast; instead of, or in addition to, periodic congregational fasts, church members commit to nonuse of credit cards.

For a resource sheet outlining practical instructions about debt management, see Appendix A.

## 6. Saving, Giving, End-of-Life Planning

The second core principle of responsible Christian stewards is saving and giving. While saving and giving are seemingly polar extremes, they really go hand-in-hand. While it is important to save a portion of what we earn, it is equally important for us to live our lives without a closed fist—holding on to more than we need rather than sharing our surplus with those who have less than they need. Saving is one thing; hoarding is another.

## Saving

Responsible Christian stewards save for a rainy day. We all have been advised to put some money aside, stash some change someplace each time we get paid, or save some money for rainy days, hard times, and when we don't have any income we'll have something.

I did not receive this advice from a professional financial advisor, but from my oldest brother, Riley, who was neither a college financial expert nor professional counselor. He was simply a hardworking man who had worked in construction for over forty years. He understood the value of a dollar and the importance of saving; he passed this value along to me.

Members of our congregations must be instructed in this same manner. Christian stewards must save for three purposes: (1) budgeting for today's needs, (2) saving for tomorrow's dreams, and (3) investing for end-of-life pleasures and challenges.

Stewards must resist the temptation to live solely for today, without caring about tomorrow. This concept seems counter-intuitive to some Christians because faith teaches we should not be worried about tomorrow because tomorrow will take care of itself: "Therefore do not worry about tomorrow, for tomorrow will worry about itself. Each day has enough trouble of its own" (Matthew 6:34, NIV).

**Giving**

The value of saving for lean times must be coupled with the value of being generous with what God has given us. We cannot become savers to the point of being stingy and miserly. Indeed, the center of our faith is giving in that God generously gave us Jesus, his only son (John 3:16).

Jesus' teachings demonstrate the ultimate benefit of being generous, especially to those whose needs are greater than ours:

> Then the righteous will answer him, "Lord, when did we see you hungry and feed you, or thirsty and give you something to drink? When did we see you a stranger and invite you in, or needing clothes and clothe you? When did we see you sick or in prison and go to visit you?" The King will reply, "Truly I tell you, whatever you did for one of the least of these brothers and sisters of mine, you did for me." (Matthew 25:37-40, NIV)

One way a developing Christian steward can master the giving principle is to exercise generosity to meet the needs of victims of poverty and injustice. Lavishness and excessive displays of materialism by Christian stewards do not model Jesus' teachings (See Appendix B).

### End-of-Life Planning

The final core value of Christian stewardship is planning for end-of-life developments. These developments include preparing financially for medical issues, funeral expenses, and distribution of assets when we pass away.

We began as dust and shall return to dust. We are aware the two sure things in life, death and taxes. This being true, Christians must practice stewardship even unto death and beyond. The stewardship of dying with dignity and burial requires advanced planning to prevent a decedent's family from being unprepared when facing a terminal illness, borrowing money for burial expenses, and the chaos potentially caused when there is no resolution about how the deceased wants his or her property distributed.

The book of Genesis includes an account of Jacob's conversation with his son Joseph at the time of his death, which exemplifies the stewardship of dying with dignity. This entire account is found in chapter 47, at the conclusion of which Jacob says to Joseph: "If I have found favor in your eyes, put your hand under my thigh and promise that you will show me kindness and faithfulness. Do not bury me in Egypt, but when I rest with my fathers, carry me out of Egypt and bury me where they are buried."(Genesis 47:29-30, NIV).

Joseph agrees to follow his father's deathbed instructions. Soon after, Scripture tells us, "When Jacob had finished giving instruction to his sons, he drew his feet up into the bed, breathed his last and was gathered to his people" (Genesis 49:33, NIV).

Jacob articulates the desire of most of us when we come to rest with our fathers and mothers. We want someone to treat us with dignity during the transition. We want someone to care and to manage for us when we cannot.

Jacob talked to Joseph and told him his desire regarding end-of-life matters. For us, this provides a sound biblical model that today's families can use to discuss insurance, wills, life support, organ donation, deferred annuities, funeral arrangements, cremation, and all other related issues. These discussions should be memorialized in writing through wills, trusts, advanced medical directives, and other legally-binding documentation.

Joseph's promise to fulfill Jacob's request provided his father with peace-of-mind that someone had the authority to carry out his last wishes. Jacob's action pre-empted potential chaotic challenges for the family to make decisions after his death by surmising Jacob's final wishes.

Jacob was alert when making his end-of-life decisions. Moreover, Joseph practiced the stewardship of caring by listening, rather than telling Jacob he had more time.

Prior to death, good Christian stewardship requires one to make the necessary plans to eliminate confusion family members may have about the decedent's end-of-life wishes. Discussions should include the desire for life support, the location of the will, life insurance policies, and other important documents (see Appendix C).

## 7. Piggy Bank Theology: Nurturing Young Stewards

We are responsible to train our children in all things, including how to become responsible Christian stewards. We do this by modeling good stewardship practices as well as teaching our children stewardship practices they can use during their youth. This section addresses how to grow children into good stewards.

Having recently learned how to ride, I was seven years old and riding a girl's bicycle when Mr. Springfield drove up to the top of our driveway. When he stopped on the road and called me, I gingerly and proudly rode up to where he was standing.

He kindly said, "I want to show you something."

Out of his wallet he pulled a new, crisp one dollar bill, handed it to me, and said, "Look at this."

I let my sister's bike drop to the ground and carefully held this one dollar bill, which represented candy, ice cream, cookies, and other sweet treats.

Mr. Springfield said, "Turn it over. Look at it closely."

I followed his instructions and all I saw was more candy, cookies, and ice cream. He took the dollar back, folded it neatly, and placed it back into his wallet.

With a stern, penetrating look he said, "Whenever you get a dollar, save some of it because once you spend it all, it's gone for good. You may get another one, but it won't be the same one you spent. So, learn to save, even if it's only a penny from each dollar. Your pennies will become nickels, your nickels will become dimes, your dimes will be quarters, and your quarters will become dollars."

This was an important lesson for me, one I have tried to instill in my congregational children and youth. The Piggy Bank Theology is a lesson for children and youth designed to create an awareness of and appreciation for how money works.

Many children grow up to think either money grows on trees or there is an unlimited supply. Others are raised to think that their resources will always be inadequate; they are left to grab what they can get, however they can get it.

Appendix D provides key lessons taught to the children at the Friendship Missionary Baptist Church.

## 8. Stewardship: Beyond Financial Giving

Stewardship exceeds financial giving. Early Christians were given the charge and authority to reach out to the world with the Gospel of Jesus Christ and teach them his ways. Acts 1:6-8 articulates this early mandate:

> So when they had come together, they asked [Jesus], "Lord, is this the time when you will restore the kingdom to Israel?" He replied, "It is not for you to know the times or periods that the Father has set by his own authority. But you will receive power when the Holy Spirit has come upon you; and you will be my witnesses in Jerusalem, in all Judea and Samaria, and to the ends of the earth."

God intends for us to spread a message of hope and a call for tolerance and respect. The disciples' message is not one of catastrophic doom and a future of uncertainty. This global Christian movement, through witnessing disciples, will result in the spread of the kingdom of God, which is open and available to all because of Jesus Christ.

Once empowered, eyewitnesses become the primary heralds of God's transforming activity in this world through Jesus Christ. The profundity of this message is its inclusiveness—male and female, Jew and Gentile, all ethnic groups, young and old.

Disciples—then and now—are not empowered for personal benefit, but to enter diverse cultures and spread the Good News. There is no ideal time to evangelize, but there is an ideal message.

The task was not conquering heroes, who march into communities expecting immediate success, but rather they entered communities as stewards, who may be rejected because of their radical message. Neither deterred nor dissuaded, they started locally and spread internationally.

They formed a fellowship of outreach and mutual ministry with a message of hope and salvation, confronted cultural barriers, and experienced religious boundaries and racial prejudices. These empowered witnesses called communities to be engaged in addressing these barriers from the perspective of the life, death, burial, and resurrection of Jesus the Christ. They proclaimed, "That which was from the beginning, which we have heard, which we have seen with our eyes, which we have looked at and our hands have touched—this we proclaim concerning the Word of life" (1 John 1:1, NIV).

Through mutual partnerships, the stewardship of this transforming witness gave power to the powerless and marginalized, advocated for the poor, fought for justice for victims of injustice, and presented hope for those living in despair.

# SECTION III

# The Church as Steward

The responsibility of good stewardship is not limited to individual members of a congregation. Church entities are also charged to be good stewards—it is a two-fold responsibility. First, the church is responsible to the congregation for how it internally uses the resources its members provide. Second, the church is responsible for broadening its resources externally to meet community needs.

## 9. Church Finance: Transparency and Accountability

Nothing can undermine a stewardship ministry faster than the perception that its funds are being mismanaged, distribution practices are questionable, spending is haphazard and does not align with line items in the budget, vendors are not being paid in a timely manner, designated gifts are being misallocated, and there is lack of communication with the congregation about financial matters. These perceptions—coupled with the offertory period being the most neglected and unplanned component of the worship service—can make efforts to move people from membership to discipleship to stewardship extremely difficult.

Intimidated clergy, who are fearful of being labeled money beggars, are often apologetic, ill-informed, ill-prepared, and quite unappealing. Consequently, church members are often deprived of thoughtfully planned, biblically based information and of being a blessing through tithes, offerings, and contributions to individuals and worthwhile causes.

In churches where the emphasis for giving is more on maintenance than mission, members are less likely to give tithes and offerings. The reason for giving is based on a biblical mandate. Church leaders must also offer a local mission emphasis as well as participation in global outreach. Notice the informed compassion of Paul in 2 Corinthians 9:6-9:

> The point is this: the one who sows sparingly will also reap sparingly, and the one who sows bountifully will also reap bountifully. Each of you must give as you have made up your mind, not reluctantly or under compulsion, for God loves a cheerful giver. And God is able to provide you

> with every blessing in abundance, so that by always having enough of everything, you may share abundantly in every good work. As it is written, "He scatters abroad, he gives to the poor; his righteousness endures forever."

**Regular Reporting**

Regular financial reporting to the congregation is essential—verbally by the pastor and through written reports that show income, expenditures, debt retirement, mission outreach, budget projections, and annual auditing. Without transparency of all financial transactions, except where personal privacy is essential (e.g., staff salaries), challenging the congregation toward extraordinary generosity will be difficult.

Over time, faithful members will become complacent and satisfied to give a pittance for church maintenance. Others will pose the cyclical question, "I don't know what they are doing with all that money they take up in those big baskets every Sunday!"

The truth is most members know little to nothing about church finances. Some people walk in ignorance by choice because they will not attend meetings when financial information is disclosed. Other people are unaware because often churches do not make financial information available to membership.

Even church members who regularly attend cannot imagine how costly it is for the upkeep of: building maintenance, debt service, yard maintenance, janitorial services, paper products, utilities (especially for an old sanctuary), church bulletins, staff, and other ongoing expenses necessary to keep the church doors open. As long as congregants in the pews are allowed to flounder in misconceptions and faulty information about church finances, there will be a lackluster response to appeals; crisis-oriented giving will become the giving standard.

Congregations informed about finances are trusting congregations who gladly support mission and ministry needs. Therefore, church leadership should have forums to discuss the budget process, particularly how the budget is developed and managed.

They should take care not to make the budget appear more substantial than it is; income should reflect the actual resource base. Leaders should remember, and remind the congregation, that the budget is created in faith. It is based on previous giving patterns and the projected percentage increase for the ensuing budget year. The church's ability to fulfill its obligations under the proposed budget can only be met if the congregation is committed to giving faithfully.

### Leadership Training

Leaders should discuss the structure and duties of the pastor, church treasurer, trustees, budget and finance committees, and deacons. Ministry leaders need to be informed about how to requisition dollars from the centralized treasury for church activities. The purpose of the building fund, designated gifts, and mission and ministry giving should be explained.

Discuss the established process for helping families during times of bereavement and crisis. These steps will ensure that the congregation is fully informed of church financial operations.

Church leadership must also teach what the Bible says about giving tithes and offerings, and share information about the impact of responsible giving. Giving money provides something tangible in every area of life, from homes to cars to groceries.

Likewise, church members should be able to see something tangible in the life of the church as a result of their giving. So, what do church members see in the physical church building?

Has the leaking roof been repaired?
Has the basement been painted?
Have the cracks in the front steps been fixed?

How is the kingdom of God being enhanced through the members' tithe and offerings?

Are local nonprofit organizations being strengthened by church partnership?

Are homeless women, men, and children being provided warm shelter, hot meals, and a safe place to spend the night?

Is the denomination having greater global impact as it advocates for social justice and evangelism?

If church leadership demonstrates these and more signs of taking care of the temporal needs of the church, as well as the needs of the people, the hand of the Lord will move throughout the congregation to empower the body of Christ to do effective and empowering mission and ministry—above and beyond routine maintenance.

## 10. Stewardship in Worshipful Service

Alexa, our ten-year-old, asked "What is stewardship?" My initial response was "Let me think about your question." I needed reflective moments to tell her something practical, understandable, and true to the biblical text. What *is* stewardship? "Well, that's a wonderful question." "Yeah, what is it?" she asked. My response was, "Stewardship is the opportunity to do good and then doing it." She listened and walking away said, "That's cool."

The deep roots of stewardship are biblical and the content and expectation is using every opportunity to do good so others may experience the kingdom of God in their circumstances. The practitioner of stewardship realizes that the resources essential for doing good come from God who supplies our needs and from our resources it is expected that utilization of a percentage is used to assist the neighbor, to provide for the poor, to embrace the victimized, and provide opportunities for the outsider in our midst to be welcomed.

These four scriptural passages illustrate situations for the opportunity for doing good:

■ **Exodus 12:1-11: Embracing the neighbor.** The Jews are on the rim of deliverance from Egyptian bondage and God directs them to gather in household clusters to celebrate their deliverance as family. If, however, a family was too small to consume the lamb of sacrifice they were to combine households with their neighbor. The whole community is called in their celebrating to remember their neighbor in the spirit of unity. Take particular note of verse 4, which declares, "If any household is too small for a whole lamb, they must share one with their nearest neighbor, having taken into account the number of people there are. You are to determine the amount of lamb needed in accordance with what each person will eat."

- **2 Corinthians 11:17-26: Embracing the humble.** The practice of what the Christian church has come to call Eucharist, Holy Communion, and the Lord's Supper has been celebrated from the earliest days of the gathered Christian community. Through the sharing of bread and cup, we remember the life, death, burial and resurrection of Jesus Christ through a table celebration of eating a meal. However, in this text, Paul addressed a gathered community whose practice denied the inclusive purpose of the celebration, for they did not take the opportunity to do good. They were practicing personal over-indulgence and in doing so they humiliated those who had nothing. In verses 20-23, Paul charged them to practice the stewardship of caring by emulating the Lord Jesus' example of embracing the less fortunate and to cease in over-indulgence.
- **Mark 12:12-26: Embracing the guilty.** Is there room around the table for Judas, the traitor, the misunderstood, the weak, and the unforgiven? Is there room, in other words, for the guilty? An open-minded reading of this passage reveals that all the disciples saw in themselves the potential of becoming like Judas. When it is

revealed by Jesus that one of the twelve at the table would betray him, "They were saddened, and one by one they said to him, 'Surely not I?'" They all asked the question, revealing the potential of universal weakness as one confronts their cross. The opportunity to do good in the midst of betrayal is demonstrated here in this religious community gathering of Jesus and his disciples: the ability to embrace your potential betrayer. [esp vv. 17-18]

■ **Matthew 25:31-46: Embracing the victim.** Reveals the failure to practice biblical stewardship does not go unnoticed by God. Jesus and the disciples are gathered during a teachable moment. From this biblical context there will come a time when stewards will stand in judgment and give an accounting of their stewardship and there will be some who did, and others who did not. Opportunities availed themselves to stewards to practice their faith through community service, and for whatever reasons, some chose not to while others chose to and did. Recipients of the inheritance into the kingdom or denial of entrance was linked to stewardship; doing good from the pool of resources available as an opportunity presented to them. Stewardship is embracing victims of hunger; casualties of misfortune; masses who lack health care, and due process for "Truly I tell you, whatever you did for one of the least of these brothers and sisters of mine, you did for me."(vs. 40, NIV)

In each of these diverse passages the opportunity for stewardship was availed to those gathering for Passover, Holy Communion, and teachable moments with Jesus; opportunities to embrace a neighbor, the humiliated, the potential betrayers, and victims of cruel circumstances; and failure to do so did not find Divine favor. These gathered believers did not have to go looking for opportunities for stewardship, they were in their midst; part of the peripheral outsiders who watch, listen, and hope will be what our liturgy says. The credibility of the faith community is justifiably called into question whenever we fail to embrace others; there are expectations from the one we worship and the community in need. The situations in these four passages reveal that needed resources to respond were available for these stewards; so often the issue is not the availability of resources, but the will of stewards to trust God.

These aren't calls for magnanimous celebrations with balloons and ribbon cutting ceremonies and high fives; just have a meal with a neighbor so leftovers won't mold in the refrigerator. Rather than personally over-indulging, periodically shop and take groceries to the women's homeless shelter; consider conversation with persons who may have moral weaknesses and fears, and surprisingly you may see yourself for "There, but the grace of God, go I." Balance your personal prayer and meditative time with visitation to shelters where increasing numbers of our sisters and brothers sojourn; give some of those good walking shoes away; be active in the political process—remember that prayer changes people and people change policy.

It's interesting to note that these four passages reference people who were in relationship with God and a faith community. It was out of such relationship that stewardship opportunities availed themselves, celebration and remembrance of an act of deliverance, celebrating and remembering the act of Jesus, preparing to share a meal right after a prayer vigil, and in an open air church school class. Stewardship is not only recognizing needs but it is doing something to address their cause and effect. Stewardship is doing good, especially to the least which validates and justifies gathered worship. Stewardship is recognizing that "...whatever you did not do for one of the least of these, you did not do for me" (Matthew 25:45*b*, NIV).

Stewardship in *empowered worship* fosters energy and informed excitement in the gathered context of celebration, which is both dynamic and encouraging. All of these wonderful feelings and energy are flooding the communities as the gathered are systematically scattered with a message through stewardship, taking opportunities to do good. Through stewardship, doing good, there are anticipated results: God will be glorified and worshipped through service; the fellowship of believers will be strengthened; communities will be transformed; and the body of Christ will be alive. The following are some stewardship examples.

**The Community Table**

Regularly, within the life of the church and other religious gatherings there are forms of celebrations such as Holy Communion and Passover. Those gathered use symbols of bread and wine to remember what God has done and promises to do. These items, bread and wine, are placed on in the Christian tradition the Communion Table. The integrity of this table is validated by providing a community table; items brought by recipients partaking from the Lord's Table by providing needed sustenance for those in the community. These items can be given to local organizations that distribute food and serve meals or stocking the church pantry for mission distribution during times of need. Every person, adult, youth or child eating and drinking from the Lord's Table is to bring an item(s) for the community table to be given to combat hunger which is a growing challenge in urban communities. The minister, priest, rabbi or Imam can use the phone tree ministry or place in the bulletin or organizational newsletter the items needed and the time and place to bring said items. I strongly suggest placing tables close to the Communion Table so persons can see the powerful effects of this ministry.

1. Clearly inform the congregation about the items needed for the month (peanut butter and jelly, condensed milk, baby formula, cereals, canned goods such as soups, vegetables, fruits, tuna, and other meats, etc.).
2. Designate where these items are to be brought during the service.
3. Encourage the children and youth to participate by marching around the community table while leaving their gifts.
4. Have a community prayer of thanksgiving by members of the congregation for the items brought and the donations received.
5. Invite someone from the community come to the service and discuss the needs of the community (3 minutes).
6. On Monday have volunteers weigh the food items and distribute them to the local missions.
7. Have offering baskets on the community table for

persons who may forget; won't or may not be able to purchase items, so that they can give financially.

8. Use these funds to purchase gift cards for local grocery stores, to purchase bus passes for local transportation, and to assist those who cannot afford their prescriptions.

9. Have a discreet procedure for members of the congregation to receive needed goods, for they are in the pews.

10. Have a procedure to inform the members of the congregation and community of their stewardship by publishing and itemizing the organizations receiving these gifts and pounds given.

11. Consider in August having a school supply drive for homeless children in your school district.

### Gleaning Ministry

Establish relationships in rural areas with farmers to create opportunities for youth to come at the end of their harvest to pick up the produce that is left in the fields and on the trees and vines. These items can be harvested and taken to shelters in urban areas for usage and distribution; items such as corn, potatoes, vegetables, apples, greens, whatever that is available.

This is a wonderful opportunity for the youth to give of their time on Saturday's as stewards and to provide fresh fruits and vegetables for those in need. Transportation can be arranged through asking persons with trucks to haul these items or contacting local trucking companies to haul them.

### Church Organizational Outreach

Assign each church organization or ministry a community responsibility. For example, for each hour they meet at the church they are to match in volunteering service to the assigned community ministry. Each time they have a meal or refreshments they are to provide the same for their assigned ministry, such as:

| Ministry | Community Ministry |
|---|---|
| Deacon ministry | Men's shelter |
| Trustee ministry | City jail |
| Youth ministry | Children's wing of hospital |
| Women's ministry | Battered women's shelter |

### Volunteerism

There is a real need especially for more male role models in our school systems. Consider adopting the school(s) in a close radius to the church and supply volunteers for the school year. Have a meeting with the principal about the feasibility of such a partnership, and you'll find a genuine welcome mat.

Your presence can have a tremendous impact as hall monitors, cafeteria aids, parking lot attendants, and office assistance and so much more—the stewardship of presence and influence. Have a volunteer coordinator, a master list for all volunteers, compute the total hour output by the congregation and multiply it by the minimum wage and witness the collective contribution you have made.

Stewardship is the opportunity to do good and then doing it. "That's cool!"

## 11. Opening Heaven's Windows

The windows of heaven are opened through responsive, responsible giving and receiving. The following are suggestions to keep the windows open:

Provide ongoing information and educational opportunities about stewardship throughout the year. These opportunities include stewardship series, Sunday school lessons, testimonials from tithers, offertory music that emphasizes giving, appreciation extended to members for giving, and disclosure of the ongoing progress to meet financial goals.

Provide the congregation with information about what happens physically to their dollars once they are placed in the offering plate. Who handles the offerings? Who deposits the monies collected? When does the senior pastor receive the financial report? When will the congregation receive a financial summary report?

Provide members an end-of-the-year financial summary along with a projected budget for the ensuing year and a letter of gratitude from the senior minister (pastor) for ministry support.

Hire an external auditor to annually review the church finances. Meet with church financial leadership to discuss the audit's findings. Inform the congregation and allow members the opportunity to review the information.

## 12. Stewardship: Caring for the Poor

The Bible speaks often and profoundly about God's concern for people who are marginalized by poverty and lack of family resources—the poor, the widow, and the orphan. The following Scripture verse poignantly represents their voice of need: "For I am poor and needy, and my heart is wounded within me. I fade away like an evening shadow; I am shaken off like a locust" (Psalm 109:22-23, NIV).

Jesus was certainly concerned with the poor. In fact, the four Gospels include twenty verses in which Jesus refers to the poor, their needs, and God's special regard for them. Consider his words to the rich young man in Matthew 19:21, "If you wish to be perfect, go, sell your possessions, and give the money to the poor, and you will have treasure in heaven; then come, follow me." In Luke 4:18-19, he included bringing the gospel to the poor as part of his core mission: "The Spirit of the Lord is upon me, because he has anointed me to bring good news to the poor. He has sent me to proclaim release to the captives and recovery of sight to the blind, to let the oppressed go free, to proclaim the year of the Lord's favor." In Luke 6:20, he tells the disciples, "Blessed are you who are poor, for yours is the kingdom of God." And of course, in Matthew 25, Jesus spoke eloquently and passionately about the expectation that God's people will care for "the least of these."

Thus, when the disciples criticized the extravagance of a sinful woman's anointing in Matthew 26, they seemed to place their fingers (rightly) on an ongoing need to manage resources to address the needs of the poor. Perhaps it was evidence that they were taking to heart Jesus' recent teaching about the "least of these."

What then do we make of Jesus' response: "The poor you will always have with you" (Matthew 26:11, NIV)? We cannot imagine Jesus was being cavalier, aloof, or indifferent toward the poor. His statement was not passive resignation intended to assert that poverty is to be accepted as a global unchangeable social system. Rather, Jesus uses this situation to teach the disciples of their ongoing responsibility to meet the immediate needs of the poor (Matthew 25:31-46; Luke 14:7-14; 16:19-31; John 21:15-17), as well as to address systems that perpetuate poverty (see Luke 11:37-52). In fact, in the parallel text in Mark 14:7, Jesus clarified, "You always have the poor with you, *and you can show kindness to them whenever you wish*; but you will not always have me" (my emphasis).

In *Wealth, North American Review 1889*, Andrew Carnegie said, "The problem of our age is in the proper administration of wealth, so that the ties of brotherhood may still bind together the rich and poor in harmonious relationship." More than a century ago, Carnegie's comment called the rich to see their interconnectedness with the plight of those who have little or no wealth, who live from hand to mouth and lack essential resources for a quality life. These poor are among us—from the time of the prophets until Jesus' day, from Carnegie's era to the twenty-first century.

The ongoing dilemma for the poor and needy is that they exist in cities and countries with religious and corporate institutions experiencing more prosperity than they know what to do with. Despite such wealth in our society, even among communities of faith, there is a limited social consciousness toward the poor and needy. A more sinister response to the words of Jesus, "The poor you shall have with you always," is by the contemporary religious sector whose response is, "Yes, Jesus did say that, but I don't have to be among those poor."

Equally as disturbing is the interpretation that says because we will have the poor with us always, we—the church—have no responsibility to them. Over a billion poor people never wanted to be in this number either, but circumstances have rendered them among the poor.

We, who are not now poor, should not boast. We do not know what tomorrow will bring for us. We, too, may find ourselves among the poor.

One of the leading charitable organizations in Charlotte, North Carolina, hosted an emergency food drive for families in crisis. When asked to comment about the challenges the poor face, the director expressed sadness to see those who were once generous donors themselves are now coming to the food bank to request food for their own families. Unemployment, corporate cutbacks, and other crises had wiped out personal savings accounts and eliminated household budget surpluses. "The face of the poor has changed in less than two years," he observed. "You never know about tomorrow, do you?"

Increasingly, individuals and families are driven into poverty through circumstance far beyond their control. Hunger and poverty will be joined together in a tight knot that will not be loosened until those with wealth realize we live in interconnected global communities where adequate distribution of resources is essential. Yet the growing disparity between the rich and the poor reveal Carnegie's 1889 call for a "harmonious relationship between rich and poor" is far from being realized.

According to the website of the Bread for the World Institute (www.bread.org/hunger/us/facts.html), in the United States alone:

1 in 8 people live below the poverty line; those statistics are worse for Latinos and African Americans. Among African Americans, 1 in 4 live in poverty.

More than 49 million (14.6 percent of Americans) lives in households struggling to put sufficient food on the table.

Nearly 1 in 4 children are at risk of hunger, and among African American and Latino children, the statistic is 1 in 3.

More than 50 percent of Americans will experience life in poverty sometime before age 65.

In countries outside the United States, and particularly in the developing world, the statistics concerning hunger and poverty are even more disturbing. We are a society of affluence living under the indictment that babies die daily and children suffer from malnourishment simply because they are hungry. We are walking down a path of widening socioeconomic disparities, with increased poverty and hunger.

Did you know that research has shown that the most significant factor in the so-called cycle of poverty is the community in which a child grows up? It is more difficult for a child who is born poor to escape poverty, especially when the child grows up in a community with a high level of poverty—poor plus poor equals poorer. There are some success stories: a few rappers, basketball players, occasional boxers, and of course, the exceptional students, who get a chance to escape this vicious cycle. By and large, however, the masses of the poor become poorer.

The future of the poor seems to be systemically predetermined by circumstances prior to birth. They are the least likely to receive or leave an inheritance, have savings and investments, complete high school or college, and become homeowners.

Until intentional strategies are employed to address the plight of the poorest Americans, the poor will always be among society, which as a whole is put to the test through its purposeful methodology in responding to the poor. How ironic are the poor seemingly so far from God yet so close to a neighbor? Pray to God to provide for the poor.

Jesus' reference to the poor always being with us is a direct quote from Deuteronomy 15:1-11. This is a passage which deals with the year of canceling debt and provides an understanding of how God expected the people of Israel to respond to the poor.

Notably, the section of text is worth reading in its entirety. Below are excerpts from the parts that contain references to the poor:

> There will, however, be no one in need among you, because the LORD is sure to bless you in the land that the LORD your God is giving you as a possession to occupy… (v. 4)
>
> If there is among you anyone in need, a member of your community in any of your towns within the land that the LORD your God is giving you, do not be hard-hearted or tight-fisted toward your needy neighbor. You should rather open your hand, willingly lending enough to meet the need, whatever it may be. (vv. 7-8)
>
> Give liberally and be ungrudging when you do so, for on this account the LORD your God will

> bless you in all your work and in all that you undertake. Since there will never cease to be some in need on the earth, I therefore command you, "Open your hand to the poor and needy neighbor in your land." (v. 10–11)

As recipients of a just and merciful God, his people are obligated to move beyond the legalistic and be open-handed and open-hearted to the poor and needy. Jesus affirmed this obligation when he said in Matthew 25:40: "Truly I tell you, whatever you did for one of the least of these...you did for me."(NIV)

The practice of helping those in need extended to the early church. Notice the practice of the believers in Acts 4:32-35:

> Now the whole group of those who believed were of one heart and soul, and no one claimed private ownership of any possessions, but everything they owned was held in common. With great power the apostles gave their testimony to the resurrection of the Lord Jesus, and great grace was upon them all. There was not a needy person among them, for as many as owned lands or houses sold them and brought

> the proceeds of what was sold. They laid it at the apostles' feet, and it was distributed to each as any had need.

If we are to be responsible stewards of what God has given to the church, we must continue to meet the needs of the poor. Our congregational resources must be used to ease the distress of poor families regarding food, clothing, housing assistance, and other resources to meet their immediate needs.

However, we must also minister to a higher level of needs, which help families rise out of poverty through job training, education, life skills training, mental health referrals, substance abuse recovery services, and other social services. Finally, the church must be actively engaged in advocating for policies that aid people in need against those who burden them.

The following are ideas to engage congregations on the local, state/regional, national, and international levels to meet the needs of people:

### Local

Gleaning ministry—going to local farms and picking potatoes, tomatoes, corn, beans, and greens—then giving the items to food banks to combat hunger;

Participate with community-based, socially active

groups through advocacy for policy change;

Collaborative fundraising; through crop walks, encourage members to walk and give;

Adopt a school that has a high percentage of homeless children and provide after-school snacks and backpacks of food for weekends;

Open church facilities as temporary shelters for homeless persons to provide a hot meal, shower, and a warm, safe environment to sleep. Consider at least four weeks during various intervals of the winter;

Use facilities in partnership with local health providers (e.g., Red Cross) for healthcare screenings, HIV/AIDS testing, prostate screening, and blood drives;

Use facilities in partnership with financial institutions for seminars about debt management, mortgages, investing, savings, and estate planning;

Have forums for local politicians to share the challenges faced by local government and how the church can help make needed changes;

Lease space at a nominal cost to community nonprofit organizations;

Use church facilities, or partner with a local YMCA, to host community hangout nights for teenagers to play table games, basketball, baseball, and exercise, and provide snacks, share a message of hope, and have space for prayer and counseling;

Have collaborative food and clothing drives with other churches, which demonstrates solidarity around causes affecting us;

Be supportive of local denominational efforts;

Consider a soup and sandwich day for homeless individuals; and

Host a meeting of local morticians to discuss challenges families face while planning funerals.

**State/Regional**

Be supportive of current social issues such as healthcare reform, crime, and illiteracy;

Be aware and supportive of denominational efforts;

Provide job readiness training and seminars on test-taking for state employment;

Be supportive of families in local communities who may have an incarcerated parent or parents, through the Angel Tree ministry;

Make facilities available to house statewide forums for community and information sharing to help shape public policy;

Partner with community colleges and universities to host seminars about aging, healthcare, finances, death and dying, and public policy; and

Take seniors to the county and state fairs.

**National and International**

Partner with national denominational efforts to be supportive financially and through advocacy;

Invite denominational leadership to conduct ministry and missions outreach workshops;

Identify a global missions project and develop a five-year supportive plan;

Plan to send church members as medical missionaries;

Recycle Vacation Bible School materials;

Send work crews overseas to develop an agriculture ministry, and then invite and host members of the mission to visit the US;

Develop a youth pen pal ministry;

Provide educational scholarships for project family participants;

Be aware of global policy and advocate for justice and social change;

Collect old glass to send abroad; and

Participate in teaching and preaching missions.

We need to establish priorities, using what we have in our hands. We acknowledge the ownership is God's, as Creator, when we give back—not because God is in need, but as a conscious recognition of his divine presence in all aspects of life.

This may seem simplistic, yet it is a profound and powerful revelation when an individual surrenders to God's presence. Whatever is in our hands, or we hope to have in our hands, must be activated by our faith in God as the Provider and Sustainer of resources. God grants latitude for usage of the same.

Being faithful stewards requires us to nurture spiritual discipline and find a neighbor who has less to share what we possess. Additionally, we can enjoy the fruits of our labors by spending a portion of what we have earned, never all. When we balance and control our appetites, we embrace caution over carelessness.

Today in our culture there is a propensity to reach into a barrel to grab what we are able to for our self-sufficient selves. However, spiritual discipline teaches the need for prayerful consideration in all situations—even during times when permission has been granted to help ourselves.

Some things we are able to acquire while other things God, as provider, gives. Prayers of discernment must be uttered to recognize the difference.

God's hands are so much larger than ours. When we honor his divine presence through faithful giving, sharing, saving, and enjoying resources at our disposal, there will be a continuous and sustainable flowing of blessings in our directions.

## 13. Purposeful Living: Priorities and Estate Planning

Youth and young adults only perceive aging (if at all) with a passing glance. Influential adults facilitate this youthful nearsightedness by neglecting our children's financial education. Too often we fail to teach them about setting financial priorities for the future. We seem to assume that there is time enough for such practical training when our young people reach adulthood. After all, they don't really have much money of their own until they have finished college and are on their own, no longer borrowing from parents or guardians. In the meantime, however, valuable opportunities to model and teach financial stewardship, including responsible spending, saving, and investing, are lost.

Even worse, for many of us, such principles are learned too late or not at all, and our elder years suffer from a lack of wise prioritizing and planning in our working days. An aged sage in Scripture warns us, "Sometimes one who has toiled with wisdom and knowledge and skill must leave all to be enjoyed by another who did not toil for it. This also is vanity and a great evil" (Ecclesiastes 2:21). This Word of God exposes a lack of balance in understanding things accumulated as a result of frugal management.

Purposeful living is not simply having for oneself and personal pleasure. This, too, must be placed in perspective alongside living in relationship to God and others. How worrisome is it to live and die troubled about what's left? The misfortune is not leaving it to someone who has not worked for it, but to someone who will not manage it.

Through estate planning, wills, trust funds, and cultivating relationships with family and friends, what was considered meaningless can become meaningful. However, it starts with the spiritual discipline to set priorities while individuals are young, if only with five pennies.

We must honor our Creator and faithfully place our careers, families, and finances under spiritual influence to honor God through tithes and offering. Let us never take our jobs, careers, and health for granted. Let us honor our labor and save if nothing else, but pennies, nickels, dimes, and quarters; they become dollars.

There are several practices we must put into play such as spending frugally and becoming wise shoppers—bargain hunt, use coupons, buy on sale, and pay for depreciable items at time of purchase. It is a good idea to have a planned investment schedule; the cost of living does not reduce by half when we are classified as older citizens.

Contrary to all the hype, aging is gradual and very real. Invest wisely in order to live with a degree of financial independence while enjoying life.

By all means, we must give by investing in human capital—children, grandchildren, neighbors—through investing time and, where prudent, finances. Those who receive have the potential to give of their influence. There is so much learned about life; therefore, we need to create opportunities to give wisdom and knowledge accumulated through experience, so others may avoid similar challenges and experiences in life.

Again, we need to set priorities and learn to enjoy every day the good Lord sends our way. Why wait until tomorrow when we have the ability to experience happiness today?

My mother made pound cakes before electric mixers existed. She didn't wait until the moment she actually baked her cake to gather its ingredients. She would take out two sticks of butter to soften and set aside the other necessary ingredients beforehand.

God has given us all the ingredients created in his image and likeness: the breath of life; a life span; opportunities; a spirit, which is holy to lead and guide us; eternal life; and a promise to always be with us in youth and aging, living and dying. *The Star Book for Stewardship* is about giving God the opportunity to use what he has created, sustained, and continually provides.

We must take what we have at our disposal. Don't curse the day you were born or lament about what you may not have. Learn to express thankfulness for what you do have—you!

## SECTION IV

# Preaching and Teaching

In Part I, we explored the biblical foundations for stewardship and giving. We confirmed that generous giving is fostered by faith in God as Creator and Sustainer and in Jesus Christ as Lord and Savior.

A Christian's belief is developed in diverse ways, but more often than not, his or her belief matures in response to preaching, teaching, and the experience of serving and witnessing the example set by others in the church, the fellowship of believers. Therefore, the one goal of every faith-based community should be to move each person who is a part of the fellowship from membership in name to discipleship in practice, acknowledging Jesus Christ as Savior and Lord.

In this section, practical materials are offered to enrich the preaching and teaching of congregations on stewardship-related matters. These meditations and sermon outlines are offered to aid faith development—the end result of which should be a closer walk with God, as well as compassionate responsiveness to community needs.

Through these meditations and sermon outlines, which contain Scripture readings, prayers, and suggested themes, the intention is that nominal Christians will be called away from an aloof, individualistic approach to church participation into passionate involvement in the lives of God's people, regardless of their life circumstances. In other words, what follows is the expectation that the use of these materials in preaching and teaching will effectuate personal enrichment and spiritual maturity as evidenced in quality Christian service and stewardship.

The late Leon C. Riddick, former pastor of Mount Carmel Baptist Church in Charlotte, North Carolina, spoke fondly about growing up poor in rural eastern North Carolina. He said, "We were poor and when we went hunting we had a limited number of shells, so we had to aim true to ensure hitting the target." Rev. Riddick used this analogy in reference to sermon preparation and the need for the preacher to aim true and hit the target.

Hopefully, these sermonic outlines hit the target for which they were designed. May they create thoughtful reflection on discipleship development and responsible participation to address community needs.

These monthly themes and sermonic outlines are excellent guides for personal devotions, small group discussions, sermon starters, and teaching settings on discipleship and stewardship development. Since all situations are different, in most instances these materials will be best used to spark our thinking and stimulate our creativity.

Use these materials freely; make them your own. Hopefully, they will serve as God's gift to you.

# Monthly Meditations

## From Membership to Discipleship

### January

**Scripture:** Luke 5:1-11
**Theme:** A Call for Obedience and Service

**Supplementary Readings and Thoughts**

| | |
|---|---|
| Mark 1:14-20 | Jesus calls us to follow. |
| Matthew 4:18-22 | Following Jesus is a priority. |
| Luke 5:1-11 | In the midst of limited faith, the benefit of obedience. |
| John 13:33-35 | Characteristics of disciples. |
| 1 John 2:7-11 | A will to love. |
| Micah 7:18-20 | All of this, for all of us, all the time. |

**Prayer:** Gracious God, for your continuous compassion on our behalf, we do humbly thank you. As we are affirming your personal call to move from membership to discipleship, please strengthen us to respect and love others through Jesus Christ, our Lord and Savior. Amen.

## February

**Scripture:** John 17:1-5
**Theme:** Reflecting God in Our Mirrors

**Supplementary Readings and Thoughts**

| | |
|---|---|
| John 11:38-44 | Witnessing God's presence in others. |
| 1 Kings 17:1-6 | Living in harmony with wings and water. |
| 1 Kings 17:7-24 | A widow's testimony; sharing food stamps and commodities. |
| Ruth 1:19-22 | Feeling bitter? The mirror says, "Trust God." |
| 1 Peter 1:17-25 | Chosen for responsible discipleship. |

**Prayer:** Dear Lord, your discerning graciousness has kept us stable in the midst of destructive deceptions, temptations, and devilish distractions. You have blessed us as members of your Body. Help us to comprehend how you are glorified through us daily, in the name of Jesus Christ. Amen.

## March

**Scripture:** 1 Kings 17:8-16
**Theme:** Obedience Is Trusting in the Process

**Supplementary Readings and Thoughts**

| | |
|---|---|
| John 9:1-12 | Miracles don't require explanation. |
| 2 Kings 4:1-7 | We have more than we think. |
| 2 Kings 5:1-14 | Healing requires obedience. |
| 2 Kings 6:1-7 | Living in harmony with God and nature. |
| John 2:1-11 | Unbelievable? Believe it. |
| Malachi 3:6-12 | A blessing plan that works. |

**Prayer:** Merciful God, please continue to practice patience with us as we overcome the need for explanations. We have learned and practiced ways which don't represent obedience to your Word. Thank you, Lord, for providing experiences that teach us obedience and faith. In Jesus' name. Amen.

## April

**Scripture:** Matthew 9:20-22
**Theme:** Faith, Being Touched Beyond Your Reach

**Supplementary Readings and Thoughts**

| | |
|---|---|
| Numbers 15:37-41 | Remembering the past, brings hope for the future. |
| Matthew 14:34-36 | The healing was through the presence, not the cloth. |
| Mark 3:7-12 | Faith reaching. |
| Luke 6:6-23 | Teaching the power of touch. |
| Mark 5:25-34 | Feeling like she felt years ago. |
| Psalm 150:1-6 | Reasons to praise God. |

**Prayer:** Lord, we can get so caught up in looking, we don't see. Gazing upon all you have done, we thank you for your sustaining presence, your available hem, and your continuous consciousness on our behalf. Thank you for reaching beyond our grasp and touching us. In the name of Jesus Christ, we pray. Amen.

## May

**Scripture:** Joshua 24:14-18
**Theme:** A Household Decision

**Supplementary Readings and Thoughts**

| | |
|---|---|
| Joshua 1:1-9 | God chose to bless them. |

| | |
|---|---|
| Joshua 2:1-21 | Rahab chose to take a risk. |
| Joshua 3:1-17 | Get your feet wet. |
| Joshua 4:1-24 | Choose to overcome the shadow of ignorance. |
| Joshua 5:1-15 | Chosen for service. |
| Joshua 6:1-27 | Rahab's choice resulted in divine favor for her family. |

**Prayer:** Gracious God, as we learn to appreciate the details of life and living, it becomes clearer that we are chosen recipients of your generous hands. Please sensitize our daily awareness, as chosen servants, towards others through prayerful peace, gentle grace, and genuine guidance in the name of Jesus Christ. Amen.

## June

**Scripture:** Luke 14:25-35
**Theme:** A Change of Mind, a Change of Heart

**Supplementary Readings and Thoughts**

| | |
|---|---|
| Luke 8:1-15; Acts 6:7 | The word of faith deserves our attention. |
| Luke 1:1-14; 24:45-49 | The need and benefits of repentance. |

| | |
|---|---|
| Acts 9:34-35; 11:19-21,23 | Conversion, turning to God. |
| Romans 6:1-14 | Immersed in the death of Christ, exalted in the glory of Christ. |
| Acts 3:11-17 | The transforming power of faith in Jesus. |
| Matthew 28:16-20 | "I am with you"... tell others the Good News. |

**Prayer:** Dear Lord, each day we realize how much you have done for us. We need you to continually stretch with us as our faith matures to Christian discipleship through Jesus Christ, the promised Savior and Lord. Amen.

## July

**Scripture:** Romans 8:17; 12:1
**Theme:** Time for a Sacrifice

**Supplementary Readings and Thoughts**

| | |
|---|---|
| Romans 6:1-14 | Freedom from sin's power. |
| Romans 6:15-23 | Christians are saved by grace. |
| Romans 7:14-25 | The internal battle within. |
| Romans 8:1-11 | No interest, no penalty. |

| | |
|---|---|
| Romans 8:18-27 | A praying partner, the Spirit. |
| Romans 8:28-39 | We are more than conquerors; all things work out! |

**Prayer:** Dear Lord Jesus, we are so grateful and fortunate to know you as our personal Lord and Savior. Our thoughts and actions aren't always reflective of our sincere and heartfelt gratitude. For your continuous grace has sustained us when we were distraught and vexed, weak and weary. We know, ultimately, all things will work out for the good. Amen.

## August

**Scripture:** Matthew 4:18-22
**Theme:** Sign Me Up!

**Supplementary Readings and Thoughts**

| | |
|---|---|
| Matthew 13:1-9; 18-23 | Challenges in receiving the word. |
| Matthew 13:24-30 | Flourishing in the midst of deception. |
| Matthew 13:31-32 | Small deceptions grow into average sins. |

| | |
|---|---|
| Matthew 13:33 | The power of influence. |
| Matthew 13:36-46 | Living in the midst of deception without being deceived. |

**Prayer:** Gracious Lord, please grant us a spirit of discernment and a will to surrender for spiritual development. As your disciples, use us to display Christian character in our daily walk through Jesus Christ, our Lord and Savior. Amen.

## September

**Scripture:** Matthew 14:22-33
**Theme:** Unexpected Courage for Unexpected Storms

**Supplementary Readings and Thoughts**

| | |
|---|---|
| Genesis 7:5-24 | Noah followed God's discretion and was saved. |
| Genesis 12:1-9 | Abram was not given a strategic plan for success. |
| Genesis 12:10-20 | Sarah agreed with the plan. |
| Genesis 16:1-16 | The God who heard Ishmael and saw Hagar. |

| | |
|---|---|
| Genesis 18:1-15 | Unbelievable. |
| Genesis 21:1-7 | It took a long time, but it was worth the wait. |

**Prayer:** Lord, in our thoughts and prayers, we desired personal and professional things that, at the time of asking, we weren't capable of managing. Thank you for denying and delaying these requests until our faith matches our will through Jesus Christ, our Lord and Savior. Amen.

## October

**Scripture:** Hebrews 11:8-22
**Theme:** Faith, in Pursuit of Our Destiny

**Supplementary Readings and Thoughts**

| | |
|---|---|
| Genesis 12:1-9 | No road maps, only divine navigation. |
| Genesis 22:1-18 | An unexpected call for faith. |
| Genesis 25:19-34 | Haste, nurtured by hunger; the results: long-term disaster. |

| | |
|---|---|
| Genesis 28:10-22 | Faith knows God's presence in our space. |
| Genesis 39:1-23 | Faith knows God is with us, as we go through. |
| Genesis 48:1-16 | Faith, a blind man's sight. |

**Prayer:** Gracious God, through numerous personalities, you have demonstrated your guiding hand in the smallest of matters. In our small arenas, we do not focus clearly. Consequently, when we enter the cosmic coliseum, we demonstrate little faith. Please continue to practice patience with us as we pursue your destiny for our lives in Jesus' name. Amen.

## November

**Scripture:** Psalm 51:1-11
**Theme:** The Stewardship of Faithfulness

**Supplementary Readings and Thoughts**

| | |
|---|---|
| Malachi 3:1-7 | Conditions for divine blessings. |
| Malachi 3:14-18 | The Lord knows the difference between the faithful and unfaithful. |
| Malachi 4:1-6 | Our place in judgment. |
| Genesis 32:22-32 | Consequences. |
| 1 Kings 19:1-18 | Faith on the run, stop and listen. |
| Job 21:1-16 | A question for God! |

**Prayer:** We seek and need your merciful forgiveness because we have sinned. Please embrace, with your merciful presence, our sinful weakness as we mature into the fullness of your will for our lives, in Jesus' name. Amen.

## December

**Scripture:** Psalm 103:1-5; Isaiah 40:25-31
**Theme:** Someone Really Cares!

**Supplementary Readings and Thoughts**

| | |
|---|---|
| Psalm 25:1-22 | Only you. |
| Psalm 77:1-9 | I'm not the only one. |
| Psalm 77:10-20 | Divine reflections can be strengthening. |
| Isaiah 40:25-31 | Wait and see. |
| Matthew 1:18-25 | Someone really cares...Jesus. |
| Luke 1:46-55 | Move from membership to discipleship...something to sing about. |

**Prayer:** Thank you for such a wonderful and eternal benefit plan...salvation in the name of Jesus, grace that is sufficient, and the promise never to leave nor forsake us in this life, or the life to come. We are excited about being Jesus' disciples. Amen.

# Sermon Outlines

## Move from Membership to Discipleship

This section provides guidance related to sermon themes and purposes, relevant scriptural texts, and content, delivery, and desired outcomes on topics related to Christian stewardship. Instead of providing outlines in the traditional sense, the upcoming synopses suggest approaches that may be developed into sermons using various texts.

The hope is these suggested approaches will be useful to assist preachers as they develop relevant congregational sermons, for one size never fits all. Therefore, this method offers the flexiblity necessary to sermonize diverse congregations.

The following sermon outlines are designed to move nominal congregants to be faithful followers of Jesus Christ. As indicated previously, moving congregations in this direction is the key ingredient to developing Christian stewardship.

## Move from Membership to Discipleship

Scripture: Luke 5:1-11
Text: Luke 5:11

Jesus was an excellent teacher, with no notes or prewritten script and no research assistant. Yet he spoke with such informed compassion that crowds sweltered around him. They knew of him, but he was familiarly strange; in his presence, there was always the desire to get closer and hear more.

Simon Peter and his partners were inattentive members of the crowds, but Jesus was aware of their failure in the previous night's toils. Simon was totally caught off guard when Jesus directed him to launch out, again, midday, with their freshly cleaned nets in waters of previous failure.

### Approaches to the Text

The faith to confront previous failures in life, even if the prospects of total success don't look good.

The obedience to follow the leadings of Jesus with hope.

The humility to accept assistance and advice from a trusted friend.

The integrity to confess one's dependence on a higher authority and God.

The strength to walk away from personal failure and follow Jesus.

**Conclusion**

The disciples followed Jesus not as mature, strong, and faithful, but as ordinary individuals with character flaws and fears, not knowing where Jesus was leading them to or into. Jesus accepted them as they were as they embarked on a mission, which transformed, and still transforms the world. The minor prophet, Micah, spoke to them as they journeyed along:

> Who is a God like you, who pardons sin and forgives the transgression of the remnant of his inheritance? You do not stay angry forever but delight to show mercy. You will again have compassion on us; you will tread our sins underfoot and hurl all our iniquities into the depths of the sea. You will be faithful to Jacob, and show love to Abraham, as you pledged on oath to our ancestors in days long ago. (Micah 7:18-20, NIV)

## Is Forgiveness Necessary?

**Scriptures:** Luke 22:54-62; Acts 4:13-22
**Text:** Luke 22:61

Is there any record of Simon Peter ever confessing his sin of denying Christ Jesus? Even after seeing the resurrected Christ and declaring love for Jesus three times, Peter has yet to say, "Lord, I'm sorry. I hope you'll forgive me."

This raises the question of the necessity of forgiveness. Simon Peter's three responses of denial as he warmed himself around flames show why forgiveness is necessary.

### Approaches to the Text

"Woman, I do not know him" represents a chaotic cosmos living in denial of a Divine Creator.

The Creator said at creation, "It was good."Yet, we are polluting our water supply, destroying the ozone layer, and poisoning the air, nurturing a war in the midst of world hunger and lauding patriotic arrogance, deception, and violent rhetoric. We must repent for our abuse of God's creation and the Creator.

"Man, I am not [one of them]" represents the denial of the character of Christ. Simon Peter wept bitterly at his self-disclosure. Forgiveness is necessary if we are to hear Christ say, "Today you will be with me in Paradise."

"Man, I do not know what you are talking about" represents a denial of the cross of Christ. Consequently, one who utters these words becomes a participant in the Crucifixion. Like Peter, he or she is guilty of self-centeredness, pride, apathy, cynicism, unkindness, and indifferences; these are the real nails and spear.

**Conclusion**

After shedding bitter tears and being filled with the Holy Spirit, Peter, as a former sinner, was empowered to tell sinners about the transforming power of forgiveness. We can experience this same forgiveness.

## Is Forgiveness Possible?

**Scriptures:** Matthew 27:1-10; Luke 22:1-6;
Acts 1:15-22
**Text:** Matthew 27:3-4

The need for forgiveness is the universal nerve that touches all flesh. No one is ever exempt from the need for forgiveness. Judas was not called to be a witness against Jesus during the trial. In fact, he returned the 30 pieces of silver and confessed by saying, "I have sinned by betraying innocent blood."

Is forgiveness possible? The last time Jesus and Judas met in the garden foyer, Judas kissed Jesus then Jesus called Judas friend.

**Approaches to the Text**

The following three elements are essential to make forgiveness possible:

1. The recognition of the offender that he or she needs to be forgiven. In the parable of the prodigal son, the son said, "Father, I have sinned against heaven . . ." (Luke 15:21). There must be a real need on the part of the offender to be forgiven.

2. The testimony of the offended—despite the transgression, all is well between Joseph and his brothers, "Even though you intended to do harm to me, God intended it for good..." (Genesis 50:20). Forgiveness restores right relationships.

3. The eternal act of God in Christ. The cross was about forgiveness, restoration, and breaking the yoke of sin and fear. All that separates individuals from God and people from each other can be overcome through forgiveness in Christ Jesus.

**Conclusion**

In his play *Major Barbara,* Act III, scene iv, Bernard Shaw wrote, "Forgiveness is a beggar's refuge.... We must pay our debts." He is correct, in part, because Jesus has paid for all our debts once for all. If Judas could have postponed his suicidal act, he could have experienced the forgiveness God gives in and through the resurrected Christ.

## Three Keys Used to Overcome Obstacles

**Scripture:** John 17:1-12
**Text:** John 17:4

How does one move through life when confronted with emotional, social, or physical setbacks? How does one press on after watching a younger sibling drown, becoming blind at age seven, losing one's mother at age fifteen, being raised in poverty, or becoming a heroin addict? How does one succeed if one is faced with any one of these circumstances, let alone enduring all of them?

The late musician Ray Charles experienced all these circumstances. Indeed, these experiences became the inspiration for his song entitled "Drown in my Own Tears" and many other compositions.

There are three thoughts that emerge from John 17:4, which speaks of overcoming life's obstacles: "I glorified you on earth by finishing the work you gave me to do."

### Approaches to the Text

All service worth doing is done to God's glory, not ours.

Service done to God's glory must be completed, not half done.

The only authentic Christian service is God's service. We are called to be partners with God in the redemption of the world.

### Conclusion

Unless one's life mission is in keeping with God's intentions, it matters little what else they do.

## Forgiven and Set Free to Forgive and Free Others

**Scripture:** Acts 7:54-60
**Text:** Acts 7:60

The story is told of a man who was plowing his field in preparation for planting. As he looked across the field he saw death. The man ran away and hid himself all night. The next day, he resumed plowing and he saw death again.

Death tapped him gently on the shoulder and said, "Don't run—even yesterday you didn't have to run. I only had a message for you."

With great relief, the man replied, "How wonderful. What was the message you had for me, yesterday?"

Death responded, "I just wanted to tell you I was coming for you today."

One wonders if before his death this man had made peace with those against whom he had sinned.

In Acts 7:54-60 we read about Stephen, the first Christian martyr. He was willing to forgive the transgressions of those who stoned him and wished him harm. Why was Stephen willing to forgive? He forgave because he knew through God's grace and the sacrifice of Christ, he had been forgiven. God, in Christ, had set him free. Not simply for his own sake, but so he would forgive others.

**Approaches to the Text**

Christ frees us for the sake of our personal liberation, so we can become God's agents of forgiving grace.

Christ frees us to be examples of Christ's likeness, even in the midst of violence, hostility, and hypocrisy.

Stephen's example is a model for creating an ethos in which the oppressed take the lead in being reconciled to the oppressor.

Stephen's willingness to forgive his oppressors, even as Christ had forgiven him, may have led those who stoned him, to seek Christ's forgiveness to forgive and free others, as Christ had forgiven them and set them free.

### Conclusion

Stephen was empowered to pray for the forgiveness of others. When he looked up toward the heavens he saw Christ, by whose sacrifice and love he had been forgiven, "standing at the right hand of God" (Acts 7:56).

## Overcome Contemptuous Attitudes

**Scripture:** John 15:18-27
**Text:** John 15:20

We have watered down our Christian faith to the extent that it is difficult for us to imagine that Jesus was a revolutionary and there were those who hated him. Jesus was despised because he represented a new revelation from God, which moved beyond the status quo, old practices, and traditions.

In verse 18, Jesus said, "If the world hates you, be aware that it hated me before it hated you." In John 15:18-27, there are seven references to hate. Jesus knew hatred.

It was for this reason Jesus told his disciples to stay connected and to love one another. Christians are not only to love each other, but also those who may, in fact, hate them.

### Approaches to the Text

Jesus never internalized or took seriously the hatred of others, nor should we.

Even in the face of hatred and persecution, Christians should remain connected and steadfast in the faith.

Faithfulness requires us to show forth the love of Jesus Christ, even in the face of violence and hatred.

### Conclusion

As disciples of Jesus Christ, we will be confronted with opposition and hatred. In this kind of world if Christians do not face opposition and hostility, we need to assess what we may not be doing correctly. Jesus was hated, persecuted, then eventually crucified because of what he said, did, and who he was. As one of Jesus' disciples, one must take up his or her cross and follow him.

## The Gift We Can Be

**Scriptures:** Romans 12:9-21; Proverbs 25:21-22
**Text:** Romans 12:10-13

Recall the last person who offended you. Think of how you would respond if he or she became extremely thirsty. Would you give this person a cool bottle of water? Our actions and reactions, our ethical and moral responses toward others demonstrate the meaning of sacrifice and compassion.

Sacrifice and compassion can be a genuine blessing to one in need. Likewise, an act of reconciliation toward one from whom we have become alienated can heal the relationship. Sacrifice and compassion can also affirm our faith in Jesus, who offered himself for us. The gift we can be brings pleasure to God and hope to others.

### Approaches to the Text

Christians are compassionate in the face of hostility.
Christians are hospitable even to enemies.
Christians are generous to God's people in need.
Christians are sacrificial as a way of life.

### Conclusion

The text calls upon Christians to go beyond formality,

even the call of duty. The most important gifts are not always material. The essence of any good gift is spiritual in nature. A big gift given with a small attitude is meaningless. There is no better gift than the sacrificial gift of oneself through compassion and love.

## Rise to the Challenge

**Scripture:** Luke 14:1-14
**Text:** Luke 14:13-14

The essence of Christian hospitality is to show compassion without any expectation of reciprocity. Christian hospitality should not be limited to acts of kindness for family or friends, or for those who can reciprocate. This passage urges Christians to expand the circle of those to whom they show compassion.

Christians should seek to do good, not simply on the basis of kinship or previous relationship, but on the basis of need. Surely, one should be hospitable to one's sisters, brothers, relatives, neighbors, and friends. However, Christians are admonished to go the extra mile and extend hospitality to the poor, disabled, lame, blind, or whoever has need of any kind.

Scripture calls upon us to be angels of mercy to all who need mercy and to be willing partners with God in ministry to the whole people of God. We are challenged to be good stewards of the grace God has given us.

### Approaches to the Text

Some of the challenges of good hospitality and stewardship are:

A willingness to share resources, with compassion, to those in need.

A willingness to share, without any anticipation of receiving anything from those we assist.

A willingness to share not solely because it is socially correct, but in response to a divine directive.

A willingness to trust God for our blessings.

### Conclusion

It was a social risk during Jesus' time to share with or be in the company of sinners, those considered of lower status. Jesus calls those who would be disciples to move beyond being socially correct into Christian hospitality ministry. As disciples rise to the challenge, human reciprocity becomes less important because the eternal promise is from Christ Jesus who said, "you will be blessed" (v. 14).

## Just for You

**Scripture:** 1 Peter 3:8-22
**Text:** 1 Peter 3:18

The unique act of God in Jesus Christ though a universal act was, in fact, just for you. Individual sin separates one from a saving relationship with God. Therefore, the apostle Peter makes it clear that God through Jesus Christ suffered for each of us, for all our sins.

### Approaches to the Text

The just (Christ) for the unjust (us).
The holy (Christ) for the unholy (us).
The righteous (Christ) for the unrighteous (us).
The good (Christ) for the not-so-good (us).

### Conclusion

This is the essence of the Good News: that the not-so-good, unrighteous, unholy, and unjust are deliberately brought into a good, righteous, holy, and just relationship to God through Jesus' suffering. The crucifixion and resurrection were just for me. Those who respond through repentance and confession of Jesus as Lord now become disciples, who are heralds—living witnesses for this Good News.

We are called to live in harmony with God and others with the assurance of divine awareness of our circumstances. In the midst of suffering, let us live with hope. In the midst of acute hostilities, be eager to do good, for it cannot result in harm.

"Finally, all of you, live in harmony with one another; be sympathetic, love as brothers, be compassionate and humble. Do not repay evil with evil or insult with insult, but with blessing, because to this you were called so that you may inherit a blessing" (1 Peter 3:8–9, NIV). For all the powers in heaven and on earth are subject to the name which saved and saves: Jesus Christ. He did it just for me!

## Lifted from a Low Place

**Scriptures:** Jeremiah 38:1-13; Hebrews 12:1-3
**Text:** Jeremiah 38:12-13; Hebrews 12:3

Recently I drove off the main road onto some wet grass and my rear wheels started spinning and the vehicle was not moving forward. I switched the transmission of my F150 Ford into 4-wheel drive to 4-low (4L), causing all four wheels to gain traction to move the truck forward with ease.

The friend who was riding with me said, "You need to drive in 4L more to prevent clogging of oil in your transmission." There are times in life when we encounter slippery places and we must switch to 4L to gain traction and to prevent spiritual clogging.

There are times when life puts us in low places. Such times of the past and present give us information and strength for the future. During these times, the writer of Hebrews comments: "Consider him who endured such hostility against himself from sinners, so that you may not grow weary or lose heart" (Hebrews 12:3).

**Approaches to the Text**

The challenges of low places include (1) limitation of one's mortality—people who are subject to chance and change of cultural ambivalence, and (2) living in the midst of the unknown, unforeseeable, and incomprehensible;

The necessity of perspective in confronting low places: the past informs the present, and the present affirms the future; and

Low places teach us lessons: (1) people of faith also need help; (2) don't be too proud to accept the lift God provides; (3) don't forget those who helped lift us up; (4) help others while we are up; and (5) be kind always.

## Conclusion

Careful consideration of Jesus' endurance of persecutions can empower and encourage members moving to discipleship that even the inevitable may not be reasonable, but be encouraged. "Let us not grow weary in doing what is right, for we will reap at harvest-time, if we do not give up" (Galatians 6:9).

# Monthly Meditations
## From Discipleship to Stewardship

### January

**Scripture:** Genesis 39:20-23
**Theme:** Stewards are trustworthy disciples.

**Supplementary Readings and Thoughts:**

| | |
|---|---|
| Joshua 1:6-9 | Disciplined disciples become informed stewards |
| Proverbs 11:23-25 | Stewardship yields personal dividends |
| 2 Chronicles 26:3-5 | Faithful stewards are guaranteed success |
| Proverbs 22:1-9 | A disciple's missions statement |
| 2 Chronicles 31:11-21 | Called to be dispensers of God's resources |
| Proverbs 22:21-28 | Careful and caring stewards of our words |

**Prayer:** Lord, as your steward, forgive me for being so busy that I am not available as you need me. Today, please create opportunities for me to share resources and speak kind words about your kingdom on earth, for I ask this in the name of Jesus Christ, my Lord and Savior. Amen.

## February

**Scripture:** Daniel 3:19-30
**Theme:** God will be there when you get there.

**Supplementary Readings and Thoughts:**

| | |
|---|---|
| Exodus 14:10-22 | The Lord provides a way through challenges |
| Daniel 1:1-17 | Different place, different name, same God |
| Judges 16:23-31 | Renewed strength for service |
| Luke 1:26-38 | Troubled, yet happy |
| Acts 2:22-41 | The journey starts at Calvary |
| 2 Corinthians 12:1-10 | Possessions of a steward; grace sufficient |

**Prayer:** Gracious, Lord Jesus, please continue to orchestrate challenges for your witness through me.

Grant me a spirit of boldness while confronting challenges so others will see you in the midst of my storms. In Jesus' name, I ask it. Amen.

## March

**Scripture:** Acts 4:1-22
**Theme:** Christ's sacrifice, our salvation, his praise

**Supplementary Readings and Thoughts:**

| | |
|---|---|
| Psalm 51:1-13 | The power of forgiveness |
| Philippians 2:1-11 | Imitators of Christ's humility |
| Matthew 22:23-33 | Resurrection is about new relationships |
| 2 Corinthians 2:5-11 | Being forgiven, we must forgive |
| Colossians 1:9-23 | Reflecting the perfect image of God in Christ Jesus |
| Ephesians 4:25-32 | Accepting God's forgiveness in joy |

**Prayer:** Merciful God, there have been situations and times in which I feared you wouldn't forgive me again. I now know you will forgive me again and again through Jesus Christ, my personal Lord and Savior. Amen.

## April

**Scripture:** Luke 9:57-62
**Theme:** The cost of following Jesus

**Supplementary Readings and Thoughts:**

| | |
|---|---|
| John 3:1-15 | The willingness to be converted |
| John 3:16-21 | The willingness to accept God's gift |
| John 4:27-38 | The willingness to experience God's will |
| John 4:39-42 | The willingness to witness |
| John 4:43-54 | The willingness to believe |

**Prayer:** Gracious God, out of your abundance toward me, use my stewardship to assist others to experience your love and generosity. With limited courage, but a willing spirit, I say, to "Your will be done" through Jesus Christ, your Son and my Savior. Amen.

## May

**Scripture:** John 17:1-19
**Theme:** Decisions and Directions

**Supplementary Readings and Thoughts:**

| | |
|---|---|
| Deuteronomy 32:1-9 | Trusting the God who is consistent |
| Deuteronomy 32:10-14 | God provides wheat, we make the bread |
| Deuteronomy 34:1-8 | Witnessing through our grief |
| Philippians 2:1-11 | Stewards of humility |
| John 8:49-59 | The task of the steward: to glorify God |
| Psalm 72:12-20 | A prayer from David |

**Prayer:** To know how you have kept your promises in the past encourages me today. I've decided to follow your direction to be more effective in my task as a steward of your resources. In Jesus' name, Amen.

## June

**Scripture:** Genesis 41:25-40
**Theme:** Stewards prepare for rainy days

**Supplementary Readings and Thoughts:**

| | |
|---|---|
| Proverbs 2:1-8 | Seek wisdom as if hidden treasure |
| Proverbs 3:1-10 | Begin with the knowledge of God |
| Proverbs 6:6-11 | A formula for having nothing |
| Proverbs 8:1-12 | Initial investments |
| Proverbs 8:17-21 | Wisdom and wealth: eternal soul mates |
| Proverbs 10:1-5 | Wealth and work go hand in hand |

**Prayer:** Generous God, forgive me for all the times I have confused your blessing with my temporary stuff. Thank you for the riches and richness of your presence in my daily walk with you and with others. Through Jesus Christ, my Lord and Savior, Amen.

## July

**Scripture:** Genesis 41:50-57
**Theme:** Stewards have access to spiritual wealth

**Supplementary Readings and Thoughts:**

| | |
|---|---|
| Proverbs 19:1-10 | Sound advice, take heed |
| Proverbs 20:11-15 | A valuable investment |

| | |
|---|---|
| Proverbs 21:2-6; 20-21 | Working hands generate tomorrow's bread |
| Proverbs 22:1-9 | A good name is priceless |
| Proverbs 25:11-22 | Better than riches |
| Proverbs 30:1-9 | Two things worth asking of the Lord |

**Prayer:** Lord, please provide whatever situations I need in order to learn the lessons you have to teach me about spiritual wealth. In Jesus' name I pray, Amen.

## August

**Scripture:** Acts 11:1-17
**Theme:** Stewards are ambassadors of the message

**Supplementary Readings and Thoughts:**

| | |
|---|---|
| Acts 4:32-37 | The beauty and blessedness of sharing |
| Genesis 28:16-22 | Jacob's pledge, my aspiration |
| Deuteronomy 23:21-23 | God's word is God's own |
| Numbers 30:1-2 | Divine expectations |
| 1 Samuel 1:16-28 | Blessed for keeping a promise |
| Psalm 50:7-15 | God honors those who keep their word |

**Prayer:** Kind Lord, you have entrusted me with the precious gift of your word. Use me and all my resources to bring about your kingdom on earth, in Jesus' name. Amen.

## September

**Scripture:** Jonah 4:1-11
**Theme:** Disappointed steward, angry and honest!

**Supplementary Readings and Thoughts:**

| | |
|---|---|
| Ruth 4:1-17 | From bitter to blessed through grandchildren |
| Deuteronomy 25:1-10 | Faithful in the midst of unpleasant circumstances |
| Joshua 24:16-27 | The testimony of a rock |
| Psalm 37:1-40 | Don't stay angry at temporary wickedness |
| Job 42:1-6 | The danger of speaking too soon |
| Job 42:7-17 | Better days do come |

**Prayer:** Lord, during times of bitterness, hurt, disappointment, fear, and outright anger, I do not demonstrate faith. I get impatient with you! Please practice patience with me as you unfold the larger canvas for my life as a steward, in Jesus' name. Amen.

## October

**Scripture:** Acts 5:1-11
**Theme:** When the desire to keep overwhelms the need to give!

**Supplementary Readings and Thoughts:**

| | |
|---|---|
| Acts 4:32-37 | Responding to community needs |
| Acts 5:1-11 | Greed and dishonesty can be terminal |
| Joshua 6:15-19 | Recognizing what is sacred at all times |
| Joshua 7:1-12 | Greed and dishonesty affects the entire community |
| Matthew 21:12-17 | When a church loses focus, it loses power |
| Mathew 22:15-22 | Give honor where honor is due |

**Prayer:** Each day and experience, gracious Savior, teach me how little I control and own. Empower me to be more of a blessing to others, knowing you are able to supply all of my needs through Jesus Christ, my Lord, Amen.

## November

**Scripture:** Romans 12:12
**Theme:** When sacrifice is an act of worship

**Supplementary Readings and Thoughts:**

| | |
|---|---|
| Numbers 28:1-15 | Sacrifice was the law of God |
| Psalm 50:1-15 | Meaningful sacrifices bring joy to God |
| Hebrews 10:19-39 | The perfect, once-for-all sacrifice |
| 1 Peter 2:1-10 | Becoming a living sacrifice |
| Romans 12:1-2 | The sacrifice of self |
| Hebrews 13:15-16 | Sacrifices which please God: doing good and praise. |

**Prayer:** Lord God, not my will today but yours, as I go forward in your spirit as a sacrifice of thanksgiving for the glory and majesty of your kingdom on earth, in Jesus' name. Amen.

## December

**Scripture:** Romans 12:9-21
**Theme:** The results of serving in love

**Supplementary Readings and Thoughts:**

| | |
|---|---|
| 1 John 2:15-17 | A permanent love in a temporary place |
| Psalm 34:11-22 | A prescription for spiritual health |
| 2 Corinthians 9:1-5 | Christian stewardship is about service |
| Proverbs 22:22-27 | When is it right to do good? |
| Matthew 5:43-48 | Where there are enemies, practice love |
| Acts 24:17-21 | Do good in the midst of unbelief |

**Prayer:** Dear Lord, grant me the ability to be a faithful steward in the midst of enemies and weaknesses which plague me. Thank you for moving my consciousness from membership to discipleship, and from discipleship to stewardship, in Jesus' name. Amen.

# Sermon Outlines

## From Discipleship to Stewardship

### From Discipleship to Stewardship

**Scriptures:** Genesis 39:1-6; Philippians 3:12-14
**Text:** Genesis 39:2

During the stewardship development process, simple, neat, understandable, and comprehensive plans aren't supplied by God. As disciples develop into stewards, no exemption is given from challenges—as Joseph discovered throughout his life. The Lord was with Joseph in a well where his jealous brothers had placed him, and the Lord was with him in Potiphar's house where Joseph served as a house slave. Even while unjustly imprisoned, Joseph strove to keep the law, to be fair and honest, and to seek God wholeheartedly, because that's what stewards are called to do and be.

### Approaches to the Text

The growth from discipleship to stewardship necessitates:

A disciple who is teachable; the learning curve is an ongoing, lifelong process. Through experiences of right and wrong, good and bad, hope and despair, one learns that the Lord is faithful and trustworthy.

A disciple who has an ongoing awareness of others. A steward recognizes and celebrates that divine blessings are bestowed on us in order to enhance the life of others.

A disciple who practices humility, in mind and spirit, not prideful and self-serving. Joseph discovered that only God could secure his future and elevate him to a place of authority from which he could serve the needs of others.

### Conclusion

The path from discipleship to stewardship is always a forward and ongoing progression toward the divine goal for your life. That was the spirit in which Paul acknowledged:

Not that I have already obtained this or have already reached the goal; but I press on to make it my own, because Christ Jesus has made me his own. Beloved, I do not consider that I have made it my own; but this one thing I do: forgetting what lies behind and straining forward to what lies ahead, I press on toward the goal for the prize of the heavenly call of God in Christ Jesus. (Philippians 3:12-14)

## Conditions for Extended Blessings

**Scripture:** Psalm 103:15-22
**Text:** Psalm 103:17-18

Human beings live in constant need of a long-term relationship with the eternal God. Behind the burden of mortality there looms the genuine desire and aspiration to please God whose mercy is everlasting. Our frail humanity generates sin, fear, and faithlessness, which render us unworthy to be in the presence of the Holy One. Yet it is the Holy One who graciously promises us the benefits of forgiveness, grace, and love.

**Approaches to the Text**

If we will offer reverence to God, we reap the benefit of everlasting mercies.

If we will strive to keep God's covenant, we reap the benefit of extended righteousness.

If we will bless the Lord with our lips and our lives, we reap the benefit of unlimited forgiveness.

If we will praise God with heart and hands, we reap the benefit of eternal grace.

**Conclusion**

Our human existence is limited, yet each generation is sustained by the eternal God whose steadfast love is from everlasting to everlasting. In Psalm 103 the poet suggests that a clear view of God's majesties may foster a desire to honor, praise and worship the God of our salvation: "Praise the LORD, my soul, and forget not all his benefits" (v. 2, NIV).

## A Ministry of Kindness

**Scriptures:** Luke 9:10-17; also Matthew 14:13-21; Mark 6:30-44
**Text:** Luke 9:16-17

Everything Jesus did on earth demonstrates a ministry of kindness. The disciples had been commissioned by Jesus to go out and preach the good news, and they were well received with hospitality. They recounted to Jesus all that had occurred and rejoiced in the testimony, but now they had the opportunity to make the good news alive in the midst of a hungry crowd—and their response is, "Send them away." An authentic ministry of kindness consists of word *and* work, and disciples must practice an active stewardship of faith in the throes of limitations.

### Approaches to the Text

Start with giving thanks for the opportunity to use what you have. Even if you have only five loaves and two fish or limited financial and human resources—give thanks for what you have.

Seek divine power to overcome perceived and real limitations; take what you have and surrender it by faith. Then watch the miracles occur!

Be faithfully bold in the midst of limitations; focus on what you have more than on what you need.

### Conclusion

When limited resources were placed at Jesus' disposal, He blessed what was given Him then gave it back to the disciples for distribution. Their limitations were divine opportunities to bless those in need. "Send out your bread upon the waters, for after many days you will get it back" (Ecclesiastes 11:1).

## Prepare for a Rainy Day!

**Scripture:** Genesis 41:25-36
**Text:** Genesis 41:36

There was a time when workers were paid an hourly wage only for the days they worked, so if it rained on any particular day, they received no compensation.

Consequently, "saving for a rainy day" was a literal survival strategy that provided needed resources for the lean times that would eventually come. A key lesson for Christian disciples to learn on the way to becoming stewards is the value of systematically saving their resources. We honor God by giving the tithe. We honor our labor by saving a comparable "tithe" for the rainy days to come. One of the major aspects of Genesis 41:25-36 is demonstrated in how God works through the holder of resources, using the steward and the resources to benefit those who are in need.

### Approaches to the Text

The problem: Lean times are real and they usually visit during our lifetime.

The possibility: Though lean times come, they are manageable through conscious diligence in saving for them.

The promise: Despite our best efforts, plans aren't always certain. The only certainty in life is the presence of God who has the resources.

### Conclusion

Days of plenty have a tendency to create an atmosphere of bliss. It is easy to fall into financial complacency when the economic skies are clear and cloudless. But just as plants need rain as well as sun, our growth from disciples to stewards depends as much on financial rainy days as on the sunny ones. In lean times, the doors of possibility swing wide open. They offer opportunities to see God working in your favor and to share what you have set aside in order to preserve and sustain others in need.

## When the Desire to Keep Overwhelms the Need to Give

**Scripture:** Acts 5:1-11
**Text:** Acts 5:3a-6

The mission to minister to those in need was not originally tied to evangelism as it often is today. The early Christians took care of one another. Their giving was not merely a loaf of bread for the salvation ministry. These were believers who took responsibility for those who had not. Meeting the needs of others took precedence over keeping personal possessions for oneself. Ananias and Sapphira were aware of the precedent, and mysteriously, they die during the offering. John Calvin said, "Luke condemns Ananias for only one crime: he wishes to deceive God and the church with a fake offering."

**Approaches to the Text**

The failure to recognize God's involvement in life of the Christian church

Our actions (or inactions) toward those in need does not go unnoticed by the head of the church, Jesus Christ

Lackluster zeal on behalf of the poor

The willful intent to represent the offering as the tithe

**Conclusion**

Ananias and Sapphira were probably withholding their resources in an effort to provide a better quality of life for their own future—but those were resources they had previously committed to enhancing the quality of life for those in need today. They demonstrated little faith and less commitment, and in consequence, they lost all.

## Stretching beyond What They Say

**Scriptures:** Joshua 2:1-15; 6:15-25; Hebrews 11:30-31
**Text:** Joshua 6:17; Hebrews 11:31

Commence any reflections about Rahab by focusing on her witness, not on her stigmatized profession. We are too easily diverted from her mission and her personal intervention on behalf of the servants of God when we allow mental images of what others called her. Rahab moved far beyond personal labels, stretching beyond what society said, to become a personal instrument in the hands of God. The primary source of information about God and Jericho as it relates to this reconnaissance mission is articulated by Rahab herself: "As soon as we heard it, our hearts melted, and there was no courage left in any of us because of you. The LORD your God is indeed God in heaven above and on earth below" (Joshua 2:11). Rahab's willingness to stretch beyond stigma and cultural restrictions exercised special fascination for writers of the New Testament, where her faith is commended in several ways.

## Approaches to the Text

Stretching to deliver the Hebrew spies and her own family, and to reckon her among the ancestors of Jesus (Matthew 1:5).

Stretching beyond stigmatized personal reference about her character to being lauded as an example of living faith (Hebrews 11:31).

Stretching to demonstrate faith through her works, and being justified by the same (James 2:25).

## Conclusion

Thanks be to God that we don't have to be governed by a stigma in permanent ink. Because Rahab bore witness to a God who reigns supreme in heaven, and because she stretched beyond low and narrow labels, she was a blessing to so many and her faith may have influenced the words of Jesus in the parable of the two sons in Matthew 21:28-32, especially verses 31-32:

> "Which of the two did what his father wanted?" "The first," they answered. Jesus said to them, "Truly I tell you, the tax collectors, and the prostitutes are entering the kingdom of God ahead of you. For John came to you to show you the way of righteousness, and you did not believe him, but the tax collectors and the prostitutes did. And even after you saw this, you did not repent and believe him." (NIV)

## Stretched because of Service

**Scriptures:** Judges 6:1-35; Psalm 78:1-4
**Text:** Judges 6:15-26

Gideon was called to stretch for purposes far beyond his personal will and capability. "My clan is the weakest and I am the least in my family," he protested when God called him (Judges 6:15). But there was a need in the redemptive community. God's people were in an oppressive situation, and the Lord wanted someone who was a prime candidate to be stretched! In the presence of the Holy, Gideon abandons his excuses and offers himself to God for service.

## Approaches to the Text

Before offering an act of service, offer an act of worship to honor God's presence and God's call.

An act of worship recognizes the presence of the holy and obliterates any excuses for avoiding the call to service.

A life of service is itself an act of worship, a living sacrifice when one is stretched to serve God's purpose.

Personal inadequacies and limitations become the foundation for being stretched into God's service and the means by which God is glorified when delivering God's people.

## Conclusion

As a steward who was honest about his personal limitations and resources, Gideon was divinely stretched for service—to usher in a deliverance of God's people that was not dependent upon him. Those who function as stewards are often times stretched far beyond what they envisioned on their faith journey. As long as there are service needs, there will be a need for stretching, and a clear word from the Lord comes to the stretched: "And surely I am with you always, to the very end of the age" (Matthew 28:20b, NIV).

## You Don't Have to See to Stretch

**Scriptures:** Judges 6:36-40; Psalm 27:1-14; Hebrews 11:32
**Text:** Judges 16:36-40; Psalm 27:1,13-14

You don't have to see to stretch, but you must have the will. In placing the fleece before the Lord and seeking a divine response, Gideon performed a stretching act. At the time, Gideon did not see how the fleece could be wet and the ground dry (Judges 6:38), nor on the second occasion how the fleece could be dry and the ground wet (6:40). The act of God was not visible, yet the results were tangible and irrefutable. Stretching of this nature is essential for faithful stewardship, for we are taught that "faith is the substance of things hoped for…" (Hebrews 11:1, KJV). The essence of stretching is never a visual act, it entails a willingness to place limitations, expectations, resources, fears and insecurities before a God who also functions between sunset and sunrise.

**Approaches to the Text**

Affirmation of the promise by positioning oneself so that God can respond (vv. 36-37)

Squeeze out all that God provides with what you have made available (vs. 38)

Ask for the promise to exceed the limits of your request (vs. 39)

**Conclusions**

Moving from discipleship to stewardship, the distance from sight to faith is elongated through trust in the promise of God. When speaking of the Lord as our light and salvation, the psalmist was not referring to the kind of sight that negates possible fear. That's why some contemporary translations paraphrase and say God is a flashlight to our feet—a light in the midst of surrounding darkness. Therefore, being stretched by faith from discipleship to stewardship, "I believe that I shall see the goodness of the LORD in the land of the living. Wait for the LORD; be strong, and let your heart take courage; wait for the LORD!" (Psalm 27:13-14).

## Stretching to Help Others See

**Scripture:** 1 Samuel 8:1-22
**Text:** 1 Samuel 8:6-9

One of the most difficult, nerve-wracking, troubling, frustrating, nail-biting challenges is to convince someone who is wrong that he or she is, in fact, wrong. To assist disciples to experience the truth of stewardship is an ongoing challenge which requires stretching.

Too often disciples are content to remain in nurturing preschool rather than matriculate to graduate school. However, the priest/prophet Samuel was stretched in childhood because he needed assistance in leading others to see. Thank goodness for the wisdom bestowed on the elders, which in Eli was stored up for the generation of those who take refuge in the shelter of God's presence.

**Approaches to the Text**

Listen prayerfully and carefully before you speak

Speak the truth even when it is unpopular and underappreciated

Refuse to internalize it as a personal failure when others reject the divine word

Leave the results to divine judgment

**Conclusions**

It is worth all the effort when we stretch to help others to see and experience liberation and freedom from the encumbrances which this life brings. The more energy and stretching we give, the more we will feel closer to the Lord, straining to hear him walking on soft evening grass and experiencing the divine presence in the twilight of a sunrise. "Be strong and take heart, all you who hope in the LORD" (Psalm 31:24, NIV).

## The Stewardship of Caring and Witnessing

**Scriptures:** Isaiah 52:7-11; Philippians 2:1-11
**Text:** Philippians 2:5

In her autobiography, in a chapter titled "Memories of My Childhood," Eleanor Roosevelt said, "Very early in life I became aware, conscious of the fact that there were people around me who suffered in one way or another." The Christian's assets of time, talent, possessions, and self are best invested through caring and witnessing to the people around us who are suffering. In biblical times as well as today, people have lived with anxiety about the future, fallen victim to disease, and experienced injustice, indifference, and ultimately death. In the early Christian community addressed by the Letter to the Philippians, Paul's language may be used to describe stewardship. Notice the fourfold usage of the word *if* in chapter 2, verse 1.

### Approaches to the Text

If you have encouragement from being united with Christ, share the gospel through words of witness and acts of reconciliation

If you have any comfort from Christ's love, share your joy in fellowship with others

If you have any fellowship with Christ's spirit, love one another with true affection

If you have any tenderness and compassion, imitate Christ in acts of service and words of restoration

**Conclusion**

If we have all these things, then the Scripture urges us in a request to let the mind of Christ guide us, in a command to go into the communities surrounding us, and in an instruction to teach others to love and respect one another. Daily, we live as recipients of divine generosity. All aspects of life are rooted in God's eternally gracious character. The stewardship of caring and witnessing is an authentic response to God's own generosity. Perhaps that is why the prophet Isaiah said: "How beautiful on the mountains are the feet of those who bring good news, who proclaim peace, who bring good tidings, who proclaim salvation…" (Isaiah 52:7, NIV).

## The Stewardship of Giving and Receiving

**Scriptures:** Psalm 55:22-23; Philippians 4:10-20
**Text:** Philippians 4:14-15

Whenever a recipient feels a gift is deserved, the gift ceases to be a gift, but becomes an obligation fulfilled by the giver. The stewardship of giving and receiving is a realization that we were all given the perfect gift in Christ Jesus, not as obligation but out of unearned love: "For God so loved the world that he gave his only Son, that whosoever believes in him shall not perish but have eternal life" (John 3:16, NIV). For many, the stewardship of receiving is more difficult than giving. We may question the motive of the giver or feel undeserving or obligated to give something in return. A gift given and received with the proper attitude is most gratifying, and that attitude includes several factors.

**Approaches to the Text**

An awareness of current needs

The will to use personal resources to meet the needs of others

Equal happiness in giving as in receiving

Contentment with and appreciation for what one has already

**Conclusion**

The blessing in giving and receiving as a steward is closely tied to the understanding of a gift being an offering to God. "They are a fragrant offering, an acceptable sacrifice, pleasing to God" (4:18c). In giving out of gratitude to God or as an act of service to enhance the life of another, the steward is pleasing God. In receiving from another because of personal need or a genuine expression of love and appreciation, the steward is pleasing God. Paul received the gifts given to him with gratitude, understanding them to be an offering to Christ, which pays divine dividends. "But thanks be to God, who in Christ always leads us in triumphal procession, and through us spreads in every place the fragrance that comes from knowing him" (2 Corinthians 2:14).

## Future Investments

**Scriptures:** Genesis 22:1-18; Hebrews 11:20
**Text:** Genesis 22:18-20; Hebrews 11:20

Abraham was called faithful because of his willingness to offer in sacrifice that which was dear to him: his promised son, Isaac. Disciples who desire to grow into stewardship must be willing to place themselves on the altar of God and faithfully say, "Not my will but yours be done" (see Luke 22:42). The request God made of Abraham doesn't seem reasonable or rational, but neither are the good gifts from God explainable or even expected. It is unreasonable for God to request Isaac be placed in the position of a sacrifice, yet it is inexplicable that Sarah gave birth to Isaac at age 90. Clarity of God's purpose is not usually given during the steward's developmental process, but the preacher may offer these considerations for future "investments."

### Approaches to the Text

Risk factor: the willingness to trust God 100 percent without the promise of a return

Test factor: the willingness to place 100 percent fully at God's disposal

Time factor: the willingness to wait, because there are no alternatives and no change of mind will abort the process

Provision factor: the willingness to be faithful, knowing that God *can* provide even if the Lord chooses not to do so

### Conclusion

Future investments provide opportunities for new stewards to learn that the Lord will provide. Through his anguish and severe ordeal, Abraham learned that God not only promises, but keeps the promise beyond the immediate blessing. The angel of the Lord spoke to Abraham and said: "I will surely bless you and make your descendants as numerous as the stars in the sky and as the sand on the seashore" (Genesis 22:17, NIV). Paul affirms the spirit of this promise: "If God is for us, who can be against us? He did not spare his own Son, but gave him up for us all—how will he not also, along with him, graciously give us all things?"(Romans 8:31b-32, NIV).

SECTION V

# Worship Tools

Growing a congregation of Christian stewards through worship requires more than sermons to get the message across. This section provides worship tools to assist congregations to design worship experiences that cause conviction and encourage Christian stewardship. The first tool is stewardship testimonies from clergy and layperson; the second is stories from the pews; and the third is pre-offertory meditations that focus the congregations' hearts and minds on biblical reflections during the offering.

## Testimonies from the Pulpit

> They have conquered him by the blood of the Lamb and by the word of their testimony.
> —Revelation 12:11

The testimonies of others are powerful and effective to encourage stewardship. Including stewardship testimonies as a part of the worship experience is an ideal means for inspiring others toward faithful stewardship. What follows are testimonies collected throughout the years from those who have inspired my faith walk and the faith walk of countless others.

These stewardship messages are captured so we can be beneficiaries of wisdom attained through personal, professional, and spiritual experiences. The ideas shared about tithing, investing, and serving God are invaluable. These are faith lessons shared to enhance our faith walk as stewards of God.

Receive the following nuggets of wisdom from the elders.

### Money, the Christian, and the Church

I have spent most of my thirty-nine years in ministry pastoring in rural Cumberland County, North Carolina. I was called to my first pastorate at twenty-three years old, without having a real sense of what it was all about.

After nearly four years of observing how the congregation collects money, I began to question dues, annual days, and other assessments collected for church expenses. When I was twenty-seven years old, I was called to develop and implement a full-time church ministry.

At that point, I had already left behind the system for collecting the money I had inherited from the congregation I pastored earlier in my ministry. From the beginning of my new charge, I informed the congregation that dues, pledges, and assessments would cease. Tithes and offerings would serve as our new collection methodology.

I am a strong believer in tithing and giving offerings as the way to provide financially for the ministries of the church. Each person connected to a local congregation is obligated to pay tithes and offerings.

As pastor, I purpose to contribute financially in proportion to the material things God allows me to steward. In fact, neither net nor gross income is in my personal giving philosophy. My giving exceeds 10 percent; most years, my giving averages 40-50 percent of my income to the church.

While not all congregants embrace the concept I teach, a good percentage does. In my congregation, more than 75 percent of people who attend Sunday worship service regularly tithe. I teach that everybody can tithe, regardless of his or her income. Ten percent is 10 percent. I do not teach this concept as a way to collect money, but rather because it is biblical.

Wherever I serve as pastor, I expect church leaders to be tithers—they help the pastor spread this philosophy to congregants. Church officers cannot teach what they don't practice.

I am grateful for the opportunities governmental and agency grants provide for community-based ministries. However, disciples in a local congregation are responsible for funding ministries through their giving. Once funds are received from every available resource, our duty, as stewards, is to ensure a proper, clear, and legal accounting.

Collected monies must travel a transparent route and be properly accounted for using the most respected mediums. I am a stickler, and very open, about money belonging to God's church—congregational disciples should know about congregational finances.

A wise pastor eliminates the opportunity for questions to be raised about the handling of church monies. It was once said "an ounce of prevention is worth a pound of cure." In other words, wisdom exercised regarding church monies can prevent a lot of unnecessary monetary questions.

As church disciples are encouraged to tithe, congregants should collectively tithe to support internal ministries and outside causes. We must be good stewards of the 90 percent left after paying tithes. Pastors or teaching ministries should address personal money management matters—many parishioners are bankrupt of sound practices about how to handle their incomes.

To reach the most people, emphasize tithing while the masses are present. Quite often, some do not want to hear it, but they need to hear it. Solicited or not, money should be discussed—how it should be spent and invested.

—John D. Fuller Sr., Pastor,
Lewis Chapel Missionary Baptist Church

**Young Pastors: Refuse to Imitate Others**

We must be sure we have the call from God to preach the unsearchable riches of Christ and be a servant of Jesus the Christ. Then we must "study to show yourself approved unto God a workman that need not to be ashamed, but rightly dividing the Word of Truth" (2 Timothy 2:15).

The church is not ours, but it belongs to God through Jesus the Christ, who purchased it with his own blood (Acts 20:28). Therefore, we are stewards and must occupy until his return. The Lord owns everything, even us. Everything we have, or hope to have, belongs to him.

We are God's children, heirs of God and joint heirs with Jesus the Christ. One day, we will be called by God to give an account of our stewardship, including the stewardship of our material and spiritual resources.

We must be ourselves, not imitators of others. Congregations may judge us by human standards, but God, the final judge, will judge by our faithfulness to our calling. There are many false prophets preaching spurious doctrine and we, who are grounded in faith, will be tempted to follow their teaching and method of delivery.

Many false prophets, in fact, pastor mega-churches with large congregations, preaching the gospel of prosperity, which may contribute to a temptation to worship material possessions. Jesus calls us to be all we can be according to the grace given to us from the Father, who has created and saved us from our sins.

The church needs leadership that is grounded in the Word of God. Its leadership must be sincere, knowledgeable, motivating, and inspiring. Be honest, be truthful, be faithful, and maintain an honest report internally and externally, remembering that we have the treasure in earthen vessel.

—Rev. Dr. Chancy Rudolph Edwards, Retired Pastor

**Do as I Say, Not as I Do**

When I played golf with several deacons and laymen at our church, I could tell them exactly how to play the hole and hit the shots; however, my ability to hit those same shots was sadly limited. This is what is referred to as athletes who talk the talk but don't walk the walk.

Anyone can talk a good game, but actually performing well is far more difficult. This is particularly true as we follow Jesus Christ. It is not enough for us to talk about faith; we must live out our faith. Perhaps this is why Paul told Timothy: "Let no one despise your youth, but set the believers an example in speech and conduct, in love, in faith, in purity.…Put these things into practice, devote yourself to them, so that all may see your progress" (1Timothy 4:12,15).

I regret to admit the adage Do as I say and not as I do was the unspoken mantra of my ministerial ministry. I never saw myself as a hypocrite, but rather, an effective leader and pastor.

After years of pastoring at various levels, I closely examined my life and ministry, and had to admit there was a discrepancy between what I taught and what I practiced regarding good stewardship. Despite my flaw, I had received God's infinite grace and mercy; however, the truth of the matter is: I was living a lie.

Since I was inconsistent in my giving and spasmodic in my personal stewardship, I finally advised the church to deduct a bi-weekly tithe from my direct-deposit paycheck.

I have repented for my poor stewardship and asked God to lead me to speak to pastors about the proper way to ensure, as leaders, we are walking the talk. As leader of a congregation, the best way to encourage people to be good stewards is to be the example.

—Rev. Delano R. Paige, Retired Pastor

**The Triple Tithe**

NOTE: The following is extracted from a speech delivered by retired Bishop John Hurst Adams of the AME Church at the Atlanta Conference of Faith Partners in September 2008.

When the scribes sought to trap Jesus in his own words, they asked him which commandment was the greatest.

Jesus replied, "You should love God first, then your neighbor, and then yourself."

The clear teachings of Jesus were made real to me by my father, who taught me the concept of the triple tithe. Like the greatest commandment, the triple tithe means we give first to God then to others and finally to ourselves. The practice of the triple tithe works well for individuals, congregations, and denominations in the struggle to serve well in the local and global community.

The triple tithe shows our love and gratitude for God and the first-ness of God in our daily lives. A tangible and visible way to worship and praise God is by engaging in the talk and walk of faith. The ultimate statement of faith: the more we do for others, the closer we get to Christ.

**Individual** Every person ought to tithe to biblically support the things of God and exhibit gratitude toward God. Every person should also give to causes, movements, and other institutions and organizations, which purpose to lift people in the neighborhoods where churches are housed. Finally, the third tithe ought to go toward one's dignity and security in later life.

**Congregation** The concept of the triple tithe can be fostered by congregations. First, congregations denominationally affiliated ought to tithe to designated denominations, conventions, or associations, which are their resource, history, and identity.

Second, the local church should give to the community in which it is located to improve the quality of life and advocate justice for all residents. The third tithe is to establish reserve funds—saved and invested—to respond to major needs, crises, opportunities, or emergencies in the lives of residents within a community.

**Denomination** A denomination should practice the theology of the triple tithe. The first tithe should go to the underdeveloped area and people in which the denomination serves to eliminate poverty and disease, provide education, and enable economic development.

The second tithe should be allocated for the international community to support projects developed to seek peace, justice, and respect for all creation. The third tithe should endow and give permanent life to valued, viable, and relevant ministries with which the church must perpetually engage.

When I personally employed the triple tithe concept,

first through my father's ministry and then my own, I found it to be a blessing. It is sacred and represents ultimate obedience to God's Word. It rejects the casual and inadequate stewardship of gimmicks and small gifts. The quality of our lives is largely determined by the quality of the commitments we make.

The triple tithe is smart because it is a simple response, which creates the capacity to cope with an increasingly diverse and complex world. It gives spiritual import and governance to our economic decisions and material possessions. It allows us to, in the words of biblical scholar Obery Hendricks, "treat the people's needs as holy."

—Bishop John Hurst Adams,
Retired Bishop, Minister, and Educator

**Why Tithe?**

In the church where I grew up, the importance of tithing was not taught. In fact, I cannot recall ever hearing it mentioned. As a congregation, we were taught how to hustle for the support of the church. There were all kinds of Sunday afternoon programs, selling chicken dinners and hot dog plates, and other fundraiser schemes the pastor or members devised.

I had been a pastor several years before I made an amazing discovery: God never commanded hustling of any kind to support his church. This realization came as I spent quality time alone reading the Bible in Pisgah National Forest, North Carolina. This was when I learned what I had been taught was contrary to God's Word.

Since God was intelligent enough to create the world, God is intelligent enough to give us a plan to support Christ's church. Through the prophet Malachi, God has done just that.

> Will anyone rob God? Yet you are robbing me! But you say, "How are we robbing you?" In your tithes and offerings! Bring the full tithe into the storehouse, so that there may be food in my house, and thus put me to the test, says the LORD of hosts; see if I will not open the windows of heaven for you and pour down for you an overflowing blessing. (Malachi 3:8-10)

Since that time, tithing has been a part of my life. While God did not open the windows of heaven to pour out all of the material blessings, and pockets full of money I had heard others talk about—God did not want me hidden among the stuff—I have not done without anything I needed.

What joy it is to wake up every day in abundant grace and mercy! God takes good care of me.

When I do not do what God requires, God is not disappointed in me, but disappointed for me. When I do not tithe, God cannot bless me the way God wants to bless me.

—F. H. Goldsmith, Retired pastor from
Gethsemane Baptist Church

**The Discipline of Tithing**

Tithing teaches discipline; discipline is a learned behavior. If an individual can discipline oneself in one area of life, this discipline will carry over to other areas in life.

Once an individual figures out how to pay 10 percent of his or her income to the church, this person will learn how to figure out how to use the remaining 90 percent for other bills. More than this, once an individual learns how to give 10 percent and live on 90 percent, this person can then find way to give 15 or 20 percent and live on 85 or 80 percent.

Christian stewardship is nothing more than a believer's attempt to obey God in the practical aspects of life. It is acknowledging God's sovereignty and lordship of Christ. It is also the practice of systematic and proportionate giving of oneself, time, influence, and material possessions based upon this conviction: all of one's possessions are a trust from God. They are to be used in his service for his name and the benefit of all persons.

—Rev. Dr. C.V. Owens, Pastor,
Good Hope Missionary Baptist Church

## Stories from the Pews

The story is told of a preacher who lamented the disproportionate number of persons becoming Christian and being baptized but did not also become tithers. This preacher provided plastic bags that candidates for baptism were required to place their wallets into within the baptismal pool, so their money could be converted, too.

If is often expected for pastors, deacons, trustees, stewards, and members of the budget and finance committees to make offertory appeals to offset the church budget. Too often, members ignore such appeals or become offended and defensive, making these petitions counterproductive and ineffective.

Nonetheless, peer witnessing and appeals, including those about stewardship, can be extremely effective. Highly respected lay witnesses are not suspect of having a hidden agenda or ulterior motives.

On every pew sits the unemployed; underemployed;

college graduates with loans; children of aging parents; older people facing rising medical costs; children needing braces; and growing children, who constantly outgrow their shoes. On our pews sit people with all kinds of financial problems.

In spite of these financial challenges, and more, our pews are filled with congregants who trust God, have tried God, and have made a commitment to be Christian stewards. It is important for their stories to be heard because their testimonies can penetrate where a pastor or church leaders cannot.

Their testimonies can enlighten church members and non-tithers about the need to: (1) put God to the test through tithing and giving in community service, (2) bear witness to the mystery of blessings that come from giving, and (3) bring home personal messages that God provided in times of need. The following testimonies are given by such lay witnesses—from single parents to retirees. They are professionals and non-professionals whose testimonies bear powerful witness to the blessings of Christian stewardship.

### Yes, We Can

The story is told of a man who died and went to heaven. He was met at the pearly gates by St. Peter, who led him down the golden streets. They passed mansion after beautiful mansion until they came to the end of the street where they stopped in front of a shack. The man asked St. Peter why he got a hut when there were so many mansions he could live in.

St. Peter replied, "I did the best I could with the money you sent us."

In March 2003, I stood before the congregation with my stewardship testimony. At the time, I had been laid off five times. At the end of 2003, God presented my husband and me with another test: my husband lost his job.

After nearly a year, he got a job making less than half of his previous salary. Six years later, God presented another test: I received a severance package from my company after 15 years of employment. No more layoffs and recalls, my job was done.

Whenever I am asked how I am doing through unemployment, I usually smile and say, "I'm fine," even though my stomach is queasy and I have a nervous feeling. However, there is one thing I can truly say—God is good! God has never forsaken me.

Matthew 28:20 states, "and teaching them to obey everything I have commanded you. And surely I am with you always, to the very end of the age." Through it all, we have continued to give God 10 percent of whatever we have earned, no matter how little. So, I can answer the question: Can we live on 90 percent? Yes, we can!

We all can. We must be faithful in giving the tithe. Hebrews 11:1 says, "Now faith is the substance of things hoped for, the evidence of things not seen." Yes, we can.

Today's economy is almost the worst it has ever been in history. There is no industry that has not been affected. Yet, our church is thriving on the tithes and offerings from our membership. In 2 Corinthians 9:7 the Bible states, "Each of you must give as you have made up your mind, not reluctantly or under compulsion, for God loves a cheerful giver."

Can you live on 90 percent? Everything we have comes from God, and we are to be good stewards of his blessings. Tithing is not only a duty, it is a privilege. We are simply giving back a portion of what he has bestowed upon us; 10 percent.

So, I charge you, my brothers and sisters in Christ, to give to God what's right, not what is left. With God's help, yes, you can. Yes, you will.

—Eddyce Hobson, Chairperson
of Budget and Finance Committee

**Because Jesus Loves Us**

I grew up in a small town in South Carolina. After my parents separated, my mother had to raise six children in a five-room house along with my grandfather. At any given moment, one of my three uncles would come and stay with us for a period of time.

Yes, at times there were nine people living in a two-bedroom house. We were poor, but I didn't know it because everyone in my neighborhood was similar to our family. We had everything we needed.

When I look back over my life, I realize how blessed I am because of my experiences. You see, there was one thing that was a key role in my life—Jesus' love for us. I can attribute this to my grandfather, a retired millworker and a Methodist preacher.

He taught us to love the Lord, read the Bible, and pray. We were taught to love one another and give. We attended Sunday school and church service every Sunday, and we always had something to put in the offering basket–a nickel for Sunday school and a dime for church. That's just how it was.

When I grew older, I earned money ironing or sewing for my uncle. From the money I earned, I put one-tenth in the offering basket. I had learned about tithing in Sunday school. One-tenth, that's all the Lord asked of us.

That was over thirty years ago. Since that time, I have grown in my spiritual understanding of stewardship. I am clear that all we have belongs to God: our time, talents, influence, and substance (or money). We cannot take anything with us when we die. If we are faithful with what we have, the Lord will bless us. We can be a blessing to others.

How will God bless us? He will bless us with life, health, food, clothing, shelter, family, a sound mind, and a job. For some of us, it will be the desires of our heart, material and otherwise. You see, no individual's blessings are the same.

I encourage everyone to try it God's way. Give one-tenth of all you have. Try it God's way and count your many blessings.

—Wendy Ladd, Quilting Guild Ministry
& Volunteer Ministry

**Teach the Children**

I was born and raised in a Baptist church. The members would march around to the Communion table when it was time to take up collections. I would see them put something on the table and pick up something else. They didn't tell us they were putting down a dime and getting a nickel back for change, so when I would march around, I would put down a penny and pick up a penny because I hadn't been taught to tithe correctly.

I first learned about tithing when my family and I joined the Seventh Day Adventist Church. We were immediately taught to take one penny out of a dime, one dime out of a dollar, one dollar out of ten dollars, and ten dollars out of a hundred dollars. Since that time, I have honored God with my tithe.

Paying tithes won't save you or get you into heaven, but it allows you to receive the wonderful blessings of God. So, I encourage you to start today and teach your children to do the same.

—Mary S. McGill, church member since 1949

**Good Managers**

Stewardship means management. We must be good managers if we are to keep order and life and reach our goals. In managing the resources God has given us, we must do so by tithing our money, using our talents, volunteering our time, and donating to causes greater than ourselves. Even though I am young student, I must balance my responsibilities to be a good steward of what I have to do at home, school, and elsewhere.

I started giving a dollar in Sunday morning service when I was very young. I never considered it mine because it belonged to a force greater than me—my parents. Then I started receiving my allowance from which I paid 10 percent to the church. As my allowance increased, I continue to give 10 percent. I really felt as though I was giving so little compared to what I was receiving from God.

As I improved my musical gift of playing saxophone, wanting to give more to God, my desire was to play during church services. Currently, I play in the church orchestra and in the band at school. Even after I started playing saxophone, I still didn't feel I was giving enough. So, I added another piece to the puzzle—spending time helping those in need.

As my puzzle started to become complete, I inserted one final piece by donating items I no longer needed. Every spring, my mom would have me see what still fit and what didn't. If I couldn't wear items any longer, I decided someone else may need them.

I also donated some stuffed animals during Christmas to the children's ward of an area hospital. As a young person, I try to be a faithful steward by giving God the little I have. I hope young people, and not-so-young people, are inspired to do it also.

—Joshua Thomas, youth

**Growing in Trust and Tithing**

I grew up in a small town near the Cape Fear River: Southport, North Carolina. My parents taught us to attend church service, Sunday school, and participate in church youth activities. At our church in Southport, we only had church services on the second and fourth Sundays of each month.

On these Sundays, my father and mother gave us—my three siblings and me—money for three offerings. The first offering was the penny offering, which was placed in a little white bank in the shape of a church. The second offering was for the sick and shut-in, and the third was for the preacher. If the church needed money for the building fund, we would have fish fries, sell chicken dinners, and host bake sales.

When my husband, Frank, and I moved to Charlotte, North Carolina, in the early 1980s and joined this church, we were required to attend a new members' class. One of the classes emphasized growth by giving the tithe.

As a young married couple, we initially said to one another, "We need to pay our bills, and whatever is left, we will give as our tithe."

Well, since we did not practice in good faith, what we learned was we lived from paycheck to paycheck. It did not take very long for us to realize this was not what the Lord wanted us to do. We stepped out on faith and began giving the tithe, including a tithe of our time and talents in service to God.

As we continue our faith journey, trusting in the Lord, we have been so blessed in so many aspects of our lives. We are not saying we don't have trials and tribulations, but they do not hinder us from giving as we are required.

So, I encourage you to have faith, as the woman with the jar of oil and the jug of flour. Trust in the Lord and give the tithe; you will see how Jesus will work in your lives.

—Frank and Donna Tate, volunteers in usher ministry

## A Youth Shall Lead Us

My name is Jonathan M. Alexander. My parents have always taught me the importance of tithing. When I received an allowance, which was not a lot of money, I would give10 percent to the church. Over the past year and a half, God has blessed me with a part-time job, and I have faithfully paid my tithes, one-tenth of all I earn.

As I have grown older, I looked in the Word of God for myself to know why he requires a tithe—I did not want to do something solely because of what my parents had taught me. Rather, I wanted to tithe because I know the importance of it for myself.

First, I confirmed one-tenth was brought to God's house and given for God's work (Genesis 28:22; Leviticus 27:30; Numbers 18:21; 2 Chronicles 31:6). I wondered about those who cannot afford to tithe. I found Scripture verses that teach God is pleased when we obey his commands even more so when we are in poverty and want (1 Samuel 15:22; Mark 12:42-43; 2 Corinthians 8:1-4).

Then I questioned if we should pay off all debts before starting to tithe. I found Scripture that teaches God is our first and biggest debt. We owe God more than we owe anyone else (Exodus 22:29; Leviticus 27:13; Matthew 6:33).

I also speculated if my tithe really matters since it is so small. I learned Scripture teaches God is looking for a willing heart. God does not look at the size of the tithe; God looks at the heart of the tither (2 Corinthians 8:11-12).

Finally, I wondered what good it would be for someone who has not been tithing to start since he or she could never catch up on unpaid tithes. I learned while we must reap the sins of our past disobedience, God forgives and allows us to start anew.

So, I challenge everyone to start today! Try God and he will bless you more than you can ever imagine.

—Jonathan M. Alexander, youth

**A True Tither**

Even though I was raised to tithe, I did not become a true tither until the late 1990s. I don't think I fully understood what tithing was all about until I was a working adult, married, and a mother of three college-bound children in November 1999. At this time, a life-changing incident occurred.

After twenty-three years of service, I was fired from my corporate administrative assistant position. Needless to say, this grabbed my attention. God began to open my eyes, mind, and heart to do things his way, not mine. God showed me how to take a little and stretch it to cover a lot. Everything I thought I needed or wanted, God showed me how to do without or with less.

In May 2001, God started me on my true faith walk by sending me a vision for an in-home business that allowed me to share my God-given talent–caring for others. Through this vision, the Lord has shown me how to truly tithe; not begrudgingly, but from my heart.

All of this is centered on giving God the first fruits; 10 percent of my time, talent, and earnings. Christ's promise "I am with you always" is true because I have now been in business for more than nine years.

I charge you: don't wait until something drastic happens in your life before you allow God to truly enter your heart. Today, begin to get to know God for yourself. Follow the Lord's lead, listen to the Spirit, and obey.

Take the first step that makes the rest of the way possible. The tenth of your earnings will become a part of the true love you carry in your heart for God.

—Stella Mack, Member of praying disciples ministry

### God's Faithful Provision

When I was a child, my parents took my sister and me to church every Sunday and made sure we had an offering. When I went to college, I attended church regularly and gave an offering. However, it wasn't until I married, moved to Charlotte, and joined my church when I decided to test my faith by giving God the tithe.

I have prayed and trusted in God, and the Lord has never failed me or my family. It has not always been easy, but God has always brought us through.

My husband and I have been blessed with three children. Our first two children were born six years apart. Our second and third were born four years apart. We told ourselves this would work out perfectly for college and paying their tuition.

Then our oldest daughter graduated from college, got a good job, and decided to return to school to earn her master's degree. This worked out because her company paid her tuition.

During this time, her brother entered college. While he was still in college, our daughter's company went through a merger, so she decided to take the severance package and pursue her PhD full-time.

Our older son graduated in four years and decided to pursue his master's. He had completed only one year of his graduate program when his younger brother entered college. Three children in higher education at the same time, Lord, have mercy! God did have mercy and made a way.

So, I challenge you to be a good steward with all God has given you. Commit to give one-tenth of your income to the Lord. You will be able to do unbelievable things with the 90 percent you have left.

Also, be a good steward of your time by helping others. Use your God-given talents to teach church school, tutor, help others with their budget and finances, or help the needy prepare their income tax returns.

Prove the Lord by being a good steward of your substance, time, talent, and influence. I promise as you give of yourself and your resources, God will fulfill the words of Psalm 23 so your "cup overflows."

—Betty Wilkins, Member of praying disciples ministry

### Tithes, Not Ticket Sales

As a child, it seemed so simple to give God 10 percent while keeping 90 percent for myself. Ninety percent was more than enough. For many years it was.

My grandmother always told me to give God what belongs to him first; the rest is mine to enjoy. However, as I got older, the 10 percent seemed to be needed for other things. So, on the Sundays I didn't go to church, the money I had set aside for God was spent on other things

I knew I was wrong for spending God's 10 percent; therefore, I couldn't fully enjoy the 90 percent I had left. For a while, I convinced myself God knew I needed the money for other things. I was a mess.

I'd tell God I would pay double the next time I was in church. However, when I fell behind, I would justify my lack of obedience by saying, "I didn't hear the message this week, so I'm not obligated to tithe." I was treating God and the church like it was a concert or show. In my mind, if I didn't see the show, I wasn't paying.

What I failed to realize was God doesn't just show off at church on Sundays. The Lord shows up and off everyday, everywhere. God's show will go on whether I participate or not. So, I decided to do what I knew was right and give God his due. I started making sure my tithes were sent whether I was present or not.

I've grown a lot since those early days. Experience has taught me that God loves and forgives daily. Our heavenly Father always provides for his children. For me, there is no excuse not to give God what belongs to God. So, I encourage you to trust the Lord with the whole tithe and be amazed at how much more you'll enjoy what's left.

—Valerie Wade, church member

## Scriptural Tithing

In the early 1970s, Rev. Clifford A. Jones was beginning his ministry at First Baptist Church in Clinton, North Carolina. Among his many teachings, he re-introduced the concept of tithing, scripturally. We were already givers, but did so casually—one dollar, two dollars, and during special rally days, maybe ten dollars.

Rev. Jones began teaching us, as new believers, the percentage method of tithing in a young adult Sunday school class. He encouraged us to begin by tithing a certain percentage of our income consistently then gradually increase that percentage as the Lord has prospered us to give. This seemed a little scary, but we decided, by faith, to follow the teaching of the Scriptures, as taught by our pastor.

It is true! The more you give, the more you will receive. We have been tithers for many years, now. We consistently give tithes and offerings, and all our needs are met and more.

We have been blessed with a wonderful home, good health, and employment. In our forty-six years of marriage, we have established a business and educated two wonderful children, who have both married and have children of their own. The blessings go on and on!

—Joe and Bessie Underwood, church members

## Listen to the Word

The offering moment in some congregations is more like intermission or a time for the choir to sing a rousing selection. Pre-offertory meditations are useful to combat the notion that giving is not an important part of worship.

The following sample pre-offertory meditations were written to stimulate prayerful giving by congregation members. The hope is that these scripturally based meditations create an atmosphere of reverence for giving; with attitudes of humble gratitude, givers will acknowledge the Giver of all.

It is also hoped these mediations will:

empower each member's awareness of his or her divine relationships with God and neighbor, whom we are called to serve;

empower the congregation to share the message of biblical stewardship and how it can transform lifestyles; and

empower members to give tithes and offerings while, as stewards, serving, saving, and investing divine resources.

**The First Tithe: An Offering of Thanksgiving**
Scripture: Genesis 14:13-24

> King Melchizedek of Salem brought out bread and wine; he was priest of God Most High. He blessed him and said, "Blessed be Abram by God Most High, maker of heaven and earth; and blessed be God Most High, who has delivered your enemies into your hand!" And Abram gave him one tenth of everything. (Genesis 14:18-20)

This is an example of giving a tithe before the law. This tithe was given in recognition of all gain coming from God and a human response in thanksgiving in a material manner.

Prayer: Gracious Creator and Sustainer of all of life and substance, we humbly bow before you during this time in worship to honor your graciousness toward us. Out of sincere gratitude, we now present your tithe to say thank you for life, health, and opportunities. Please accept this tithe and contribution as a thank-you offering. In your name we pray. Amen!

**The Tithe: A Response to God's Blessings**
Scripture: Genesis 28:16-22

> Then Jacob made a vow, saying, "If God will be with me and will watch over me on this journey I am taking and will give me food to eat and clothes to wear so that I return safely to my father's house, then the LORD will be my God and this stone that I have set up as a pillar will be God's house, and of all that you give me I will give you a tenth." (Genesis 28:20-22, NIV)

Before the letter of the law, Jacob responds to God's personal generosity towards his life. He realized that ultimate personal security was dependent upon God, and a fitting response to such gracious and divine generosity was a personal tithe set aside in gratitude for God's purpose.

Prayer: O Lord God, we could never repay you for all you have done, are doing, and have promised to do with and in our lives. Continuously, new blessings are showered upon us. At this very moment, we are reaping our blessings. Please accept our tithe and contribution in grateful gratitude for your blessings. Thank you so much! Amen.

## The Poor Are Blessed through the Tithe

Scripture: Deuteronomy 14:28-29

> At the end of every three years, bring all the tithes of that year's produce and store it in your towns, so that the Levites (who have no allotment or inheritance of their own) and the foreigners, the fatherless and the widows who live in your towns may come and eat and be satisfied, and so that the LORD your God may bless you in all the work of your hands. (Deuteronomy 14:28-29, NIV)

The tithe was God's gift to the poor. Consequently, as one fails to tithe, the poor, fatherless, widowed, homeless, hungry, naked, and imprisoned are neglected by the religious community. God will bless the endeavors of all those who remember the least and lost.

Prayer: Lord, in the midst of plenty there are those who have not. As recipients of plenty, please remove from us the spirits of arrogance, self-centeredness, greed, and selfishness. Give eyes to see, ears to hear, and a heart of compassion that cause the plenty we enjoy to be enjoyed by the least and lost. Amen.

**Relationship to God Should Not Depend on Health or Wealth**
Scripture: Job 1:13-22

> [Job] said, "Naked I came from my mother's womb, and naked shall I return there; the LORD gave, and the LORD has taken away; blessed be the name of the LORD." (Job 1:21)

All life begins with a breath of life and ceases when breath departs. In a pure sense, we begin life without possessions. Even possessions placed into caskets are of no use to decedents. Discover the essence and joy of life in the presence or absence of things. An eternal relationship with the eternal is nurtured regularly by saying with Job, "blessed be the name of the LORD."

Prayer: You are the gracious giver of life, O God. Yet, too often we encounter your gift by diluting its significance with meaningless material things we allow to define our lives. Please forgive us for the sins of greed, selfishness, excessive want, hoarding resources, and living a superficial lifestyle—all of which are temporary. Your name be blessed, for our hope is in you. Amen.

**Trust in the Lord Is Validated by Doing Good**
Scripture: Psalm 37:2-7

> Trust in the LORD and do good; …
> Take delight in the LORD,
> and he will give you the desires of your heart.
> Commit your way to the LORD;
> trust in him and he will do this: …
> Be still before the LORD and wait patiently
> for him.…
> —Psalm 37:3*a*, 4-5, 7*a*, NIV

One of the greatest challenges throughout our lives is to trust ourselves, others, and God. We are challenged daily as we wait on many things, including God. We often order God to do what we want, right now. Appreciating God, others, and ourselves requires trust that doing good and giving is nurtured by trust in God.

Prayer: Lord, we are learning each day, through each challenging obstacle and disappointment, to trust you more. Being empowered through trust, we are learning to patiently seek your will for our lives, then being accessible to do godly good. Amen.

**This Scripture Never Said the People Weren't Giving**
Scripture: Malachi 3:8

> Will anyone rob God? Yet you are robbing me! But you say, "How are we robbing you?" In your tithes and offerings! (Malachi 3:8)

It is impossible to rob God, directly. People of faith indirectly rob God whenever we claim ownership of our earnings and determine how much we choose to give back. This indictment is not one of failure to give, but failure to give as directed by God. God is robbed every time a believer functions financially independent of the divine directive to give tithes and offerings.

Prayer: Ten percent of our gross income may be a lot of money, Lord. We never thought in terms of being a robber, mainly because we looked at it as our money. So, we gave—sometimes. Now, we understand ours is really yours and you ultimately gave us all. Gladly we bring our tithe and contribution. Please forgive us of past trespasses. Amen.

**Jesus Affirms the Law and Prophets, but Denounced Legalism**
Scripture: Matthew 5:17-20

> "Anyone who breaks one of the least of these commandments and teaches others accordingly will be called least in the kingdom of heaven, but whoever practices and teaches these commands will be called great in the kingdom of heaven. For I tell you that unless your righteousness surpasses that of the Pharisees and the teachers of the law, you will certainly not enter the kingdom of heaven." (Matthew 5:19-20, NIV)

The kingdom of heaven and the earth are becoming the kingdom of God. To be sure, it is not a kingdom of legalism. Jesus was clear his mission was not one of destroying the Law and Prophets. In fact, a terse warning is given in reference to breaking the Law. However, Jesus calls believers to exceed the narrow parameters of legalism to a broader field of love, mercy, justice, love, and caring.

Prayer: Lord Jesus, thank you for intentionally moving the practice of faith beyond legalism, while not destroying the intent and purpose of the obligation of giving tithes and contributions; not because the Law states it, but because love demands it. Amen.

**Locate Your Treasure and Find Your Heart**
Scripture: Matthew 6:19-30

> "For where your treasure is, there your heart will be also." (Matthew 6:21, NIV)

There is absolutely nothing sinful about saving and investing, but remember these things. God has given you life and will also provide the necessities to sustain life (v. 25). God daily feeds the birds and clothes the flowers; and you are created in God's image, so stop worrying about stuff (vv. 26, 28-30). All anxious care and worry about attainable things is unnecessary because all is unattainable without divine blessings (v. 27). Such feelings of worry, anxiousness for tomorrow's good, hoarding God's treasure, and self-centeredness are not attributes of a child of God (vv. 31-32).

Prayer: Gracious Lord, we become agitated and anxious when life situations don't occur in a reasonable time frame. Your Word helps us to develop a better perspective on what our priorities should be. Lord,it is clear where our heart is by the way we allocate our treasures. In Jesus' name! Amen.

**Give until It Feels Godly**
Scripture: Luke 6:37-38

> "Give, and it will be given to you. A good measure, pressed down, shaken together and running over, will be poured into your lap. For with the measure you use, it will be measured to you." (Luke 6:38, NIV)

Five reasons a believer cannot afford to not give:

All an individual has is a direct result of divine goodness and divine generosity—"Every good gift is from above."

Ultimately, all one possesses is the Lord's. "All things come of thee, O Lord, and of thine own have we given thee."

The tithe and contribution are holy unto the Lord. "The tithe is the Lord's."

Christians have the mind of Christ, which compels outreach through giving tithes and offerings. "Let this mind be in you which was also in Christ Jesus."

Jesus promises to give to all who give, "Give, and it will be given to you."

Prayer: Dearest Christ, as recipients of grace to be generous, teach us to be loving and caring toward others in giving tithes and contributions. You have been so faithful toward us. Use us today to bring blessing of good tidings and immense joy to others today, in Jesus' name. Amen.

**They Graciously Gave and Received**
Scripture: Acts 2:42-47

> All who believed were together and had all things in common; they would sell their possessions and goods and distribute the proceeds to all, as any had need. (Acts 2:44-45)

Unselfish and reciprocated kindness was the permanent glue that solidified the fresh fellowship of early Christians. They acknowledged the grace extended to them through Jesus Christ by responding to the needs of the poor.

Those who believed and trusted in Jesus had not only faith in common, but an inclusive fellowship with the poor. Needs within this fellowship demanded a response beyond tithes and offerings. Their giving was not rooted in legalism, but was a willing and loving response to God's grace. Experience the grace of God through giving that begins, not ends, with the tithe.

Prayer: Lord, thank you for showing us how to respond to needs. Grant us today, Lord, more compassion and will to address the needs of our day. May we show your kingdom on earth through our genuine outreach to our brothers and sisters. In Jesus' name we pray. Amen.

**Smile While Giving God's Tithe and Offering**
Scripture: 2 Corinthians 9:6-9

> The point is this: the one who sows sparingly will also reap sparingly, and the one who sows bountifully will also reap bountifully. Each of you must give as you have made up your mind, not reluctantly or under compulsion, for God loves a cheerful giver. (2 Corinthians 9:6-7)

Sowing and reaping is the equivalent of giving and receiving. Persons in relationship with God have the promise of receiving in direct proportion to their giving. The more given in tithes and contributions, the more needs can be addressed for the poor and needy.

Giving, however, should never be the basis for receiving as much or more in return for what has been given. In fact, the only return may be in making God happy. For God loves a cheerful giver. Therefore, be a blessing and cause others to be cheerful through your generosity.

Prayer: Lord Jesus, we thank you for loving us more than we have shown toward you and others. We confess there have been times our attitudes and dispositions were not cheerful during the offertory period of worship. We want to make you smile by making those who are in need smile as a result of our cheerful giving. Amen.

**Wealth—We Can't Take It with Us**
Scripture: 1 Timothy 6:6-19

> For we brought nothing into the world, and we can take nothing out of it....For the love of money is a root of all kinds of evil. Some people, eager for money, have wandered from the faith and pierced themselves with many griefs (1 Timothy 6:7,10, NIV).

The love of money is a root of all kinds of evil. Evils that occur from loving money are: self-centeredness, greed, false trust, independence from God, worry about keeping and gaining wealth, arrogance, indifference to the poor, unsatisfied desires, bondage in wealth pursuits, and failure to tithe.

Money, wealth, and assets aren't evil in and of themselves. The danger is when we make the pursuit of wealth an intense focus in life. Wealth—we can send some ahead, leave some behind, but we can't take it with us. At the end of the day, whether or not we have little or much, life's ultimate goal should be inward contentment and peace with God.

Prayer: Comparatively speaking, Lord, to some I am poor; to others I am wealthy. Thank you for wealth and through it the ability to address numerous needs of homeless children, victims of injustice—all who have needs. Lord Jesus, because of you, all of us can have the same thing: eternal life through faith in you. It's affordable to all because you paid the price. Thank you! Amen.

A P P E N D I X  A

# Stewardship through Debt

## 1. Personal Accountability

You cannot borrow your way out of debt.

Know the difference between good and bad debt. Good debt is incurred on items that increase in value (e.g., houses, education); bad debt is accumulated on items that decrease in value (e.g., cars, clothes).

Make sure your expenditures are essential. If you don't need it, don't buy it, especially if you cannot afford it.

Know all of your sources of income.

## 2. Instructional Steps

Structure expenditures around essential expenses—write them down or enter them into the computer. Be clear about the difference between need and want.

Balance income and expenditures—income should be more than expenditures. For example, if income is $20,000 per year, expenses should not exceed $19,500 per year. Write income-expenditure comparisons down to review weekly and monthly.

Write down sources of income and all expenses; set priorities for resource usage, starting with essentials.

Credit cards aren't bad; the real issue is undisciplined management and usage. Wherever possible, with credit card debt, restructure to the lowest available interest.

Debt management demands setting priorities for essential expenses to handle debt. Resources must be set aside and paid in a timely manner to reduce debt. Be sure that you always pay more than the interest and minimum payment.

**3. Consistently Manage Your Finances**

Balance and reconcile your bank statement and checkbook.

Monitor expenses weekly, especially miscellaneous expenses: eating out, buying non-essential sale items, etc.

Pay bills on time to avoid penalties and interest.

**4. The Goals of Debt Management**

To live without financial constraints to enjoy each day as God's blessing.

To understand the difference between essentials and wants then set priorities for the same.

To regularly balance income and expenditures.

To eventually have savings and investments.

To contribute resources, time, and influence to enhance the lives of others.

To hear the words: "His master replied, 'Well done, good and faithful servant! You have been faithful with a few things; I will put you in charge of many things. Come and share your master's happiness!'" (Matthew 25:21, NIV).

# APPENDIX B

# Stewardship through Saving and Giving

## To Give and Save One Must Cease

Immediate gratification for good deeds.

Saying, "I don't have enough to save, nor time to give."

Expecting a plaque or honorarium for services given.

Being one of the following individuals

- A person who doesn't give to anything or anyone;
- A person who only tithes to the church; and
- A person who gives for personal recognition.

## One Who Desires to Give and Save Must

Develop a savings and spending plan.

Decide where you want your money to go.

Decide how much you want to save and invest.

## Consider the 10.10.80 Plan

Give 10 percent of your finances to church, and time in volunteer services.

Save 10 percent toward future expenses or emergencies.

Live on 80 percent or less of household finances.

**Implement wise financial practices**

Don't be embarrassed to use coupons.

Take advantage of sales and discount offers.

Eat out less, cook at home more.

Learn to say no!

**Use credit wisely**

Charge what you can pay in thirty days.

Pay on time to eliminate late fees.

Understand issuer terms (annual fees and interest rates) before you activate the card.

Regularly review giving and savings plan to identify spending leaks and repair them immediately.

**The Goals of Giving and Saving**

To pay all monthly expenditures and have savings.

To give the Lord's tithe and offering.

To meet short-term goals (six months); intermediate goals (six months to three years); and long-term goals (three years and beyond).

To live with less stress about possible financial crises.

To give and save in such a manner to hear, "Servant, well done."

# APPENDIX C

# End-of-Life Stewardship

**The stewardship of aging requires the following acknowledgments:**

The gift of life is the most precious gift you will ever receive; be a good steward of your health.

The length of life is not guaranteed; learn to enjoy today.

The cost of living, the cost of healthcare, and the cost of dying increases every year.

The desired peace of mind at the end of life requires planning.

All who live will die.

**A Good Steward through End-of-Life Matters Must:**

Have a discussion with their estate executor, attorney-in-fact, and family members about long-term care and life support.

Have a discussion to plan personal asset management, and when and which conditions determine management responsibilities need to be relinquished, and who is designated to take over.

Have a plan for the distribution of personal items to individuals and organizations before death.

Have a financial plan for end-of-life challenges; start saving and investing now.

Have a discussion with immediate family—spouse, children, grandchildren, siblings, etc. about end-of-life desires. If necessary, put your desires in writing.

Have a will with designated power of attorney, an executor, who will carry out your wishes. It should also include wishes about organ donation, disbursement of assets, and provisions to contribute to your church, mosque, synagogue, or other religious organization.

**The Goals of End-of-Life Stewardship Matters:**

To enjoy the cost of living and predetermine how much I am willing to pay for end-of-life challenges;

To tithe after death through a deferred giving plan;

To discuss my expectations with family members or a caretaker about my end-of-life challenges;

To determine if and under what conditions I desire life support;

To plan my funeral service;

To have peace of mind, enjoying today, having prepared for the cost of tomorrow's transition.

## APPENDIX D

# Growing Young Stewards

## Children

### To Develop into Young Stewards, Children and Youth Must Realize:

Parents need money to buy clothes, shoes, and school supplies.

French fries, ice cream, video games, and books cost money.

Having money is hard work.

Feed your piggy bank its favorite food—money.

### Young Stewards Must Understand:

Ways to get money:

Earnings: be sure to do the chores your parents tell you to do.

Allowance: the money your parents give you to save and spend.

Gifts: the occasional money you receive from relatives and friends.

Things to save for:

College

Car and car insurance

Future home

Things to spend for:

Books, so you can read about people, places, and things

Toys

Snacks and activities

Things to share by giving:

Become an advocate for school-age children who are homeless or impoverished.

Coordinate a Christmas party for homeless children from your school.

Develop a pen pal relationship with children in a school from Haiti and have a school supply drive.

**The Goals to Growing Young Stewards:**

To inform children about money

To create an interest in understanding how money works

To create a spirit of responsiveness to the needs of less fortunate children

To instill thinking before children spend their money

To develop good saving habits

## Teenagers

**To Become Good Stewards, Teens Must Resist:**

Signing up for or accepting credit card applications.

Maxing out debit card limit.

Spending entire allowance or money earned from a part-time job.

Borrowing from or lending money to friends.

Excessive purchases on fast food, designer clothes, and other luxuries.

**A Good Teen Steward Must:**

Grasp the meaning of income and expenses

Learn the difference between gross income and net pay

Learn about federal and state taxes, healthcare contributions, and other deductions from a paycheck

Plan a budget based on net pay

Open a personal savings or checking account

Know how to reconcile bank statements on a monthly basis

Understand depreciation related to items purchased

Understand payment terms, interest rate, late charges, and other fees before applying for a credit card;

Recognize that items charged today have to be paid tomorrow.

**The Goals of Good Teen Stewardship:**

To learn the importance of money management;

To have some savings to assist with short-term goals;

To honor God through giving the tithe;

To learn the importance of balancing expenditures for oneself and others;

To have disposable income to engage in enjoyable activities.

# For Every Minister's Library

## The Star Book on Preaching

Marvin A. McMickle

In the classic tradition of *The Star Book for Ministers*, Judson Press offers this Star Book with a special focus on preaching. Without an emphasis toward any denomination and practical in its nature, the guide offers:

- keys to an effective preaching ministry, including goals and outcomes of preaching
- text and topic selection
- information on various types of sermons
- a look at different preaching styles such as narrative and first-person preaching
- suggestions for sermon preparation
- ideas for several sermon series
- a full list of preaching resources to use as references

*The Star Book on Preaching* also features more than a dozen sermon outlines on various topics, addressing:

- developing key points and direction
- effective introductions and closings
- style and delivery

Hardcover, 978-0-8170-1492-6 $15.00

800-458-3766 / www.judsonpress.com